Praise for *The Essentials of Business Etiquette*

"If you are looking for practical guidelines on how to conduct yourself in a business situation, what behaviors you need to use to get ahead, and how to be sure that you do not offend others, read this book!"—Madeline Bell, President and COO, The Children's Hospital of Philadelphia

"Pachter has once again done an excellent job at highlighting some key tools to succeed in leadership and how to conduct yourself in the workplace."—Joseph A. Barone, PharmD, FCCP, Dean and Professor II, Rutgers University, Ernest Mario School of Pharmacy

"The pragmatic advice Barbara offers is sure to meaningfully help people be more confident and effective in multiple business situations."—Elizabeth Walker, Vice President, Global Talent Management, Campbell Soup Company

Praise for *The Power of Positive Confrontation, First Edition*

Barbara Pachter has written a wonderfully perceptive and incredibly constructive book. Instead of complaining when someone does something that annoys you, now you'll know the basic strategies for handling conflict effectively while feeling good about the experience. Everyone needs to read this book!—Sharon J. Wohlmuth, *New York Times* best-selling co-author of Sisters, Mothers and Daughters, and Best Friends

This is one of the best self-help books ever written. I wish this wonderful book had been available to me long ago—it would have saved me years of problems. We face the problems it identifies daily. The help it offers is immediate.—Larry King, Hall of Fame Broadcaster

THE POWER OF
POSITIVE
CONFRONTATION

Also by Barbara Pachter

The Essentials of Business Etiquette:
How to Greet, Eat, and Tweet Your Way to Success

New Rules @ Work:
79 Etiquette Tips, Tools, and Techniques to Get Ahead and Stay Ahead

When the Little Things Count . . . and They Always Count:
601 Essential Things That Everyone in Business Needs to Know

The Jerk with the Cell Phone:
A Survival Guide for the Rest of Us

Minding Your Business Manners

Prentice Hall Complete Business Etiquette Handbook

Business Etiquette

Climbing the Corporate Ladder:
What You Need to Know and Do to Be a Promotable Person

**COMPLETELY REVISED
and UPDATED EDITION**

THE POWER OF
POSITIVE
CONFRONTATION

THE SKILLS YOU NEED
TO HANDLE CONFLICTS
at WORK, *at* HOME,
ONLINE, *and* IN LIFE

BARBARA PACHTER
with SUSAN MAGEE

Da Capo
LIFE
LONG

A Member of the Perseus Books Group

Book design by Cynthia Young

Pachter, Barbara.
   The power of positive confrontation : the skills you need to handle conflicts at work,
   at home, online, and in life / by Barbara Pachter with Susan Magee.
     pages cm

   ISBN 978-0-7382-1759-8 (pbk.) — ISBN 978-0-7382-1760-4 (e-book)
   1. Interpersonal conflict.   2. Interpersonal confrontation.   I. Magee, Susan.   II. Title.

BF637.I48P33 2014

158.2—dc23

                                                            2014005086

First Da Capo Press Edition 2014
Published by Da Capo Press
A Member of the Perseus Books Group
www.dacapopress.com

Da Capo Press books are available at special discounts for bulk purchases in the U.S. by corporations, institutions, and other organizations. For more information, please contact the Special Markets Department at the Perseus Books Group, 2300 Chestnut Street, Suite 200, Philadelphia, PA, 19103, or call (800) 810-4145, ext. 5000, or e-mail special.markets@ perseusbooks.com.

10 9 8 7 6 5 4 3

To the memory of my parents, Esther and Victor Pachter.

CONTENTS

PART III

Conflict-Free Living

INTRODUCTION

For more than twenty years I've been a business communications trainer and coach specializing in communication and etiquette skills. Practically since the day I started, I've had participants make comments during my seminars, or come up to me at breaks or after workshop sessions to share their experiences with someone they were having difficulty with. My seminar participants have come from all walks of life and all levels of the corporate food chain—from senior VPs at Fortune 500 companies to administrative assistants in accounting firms. Again and again, these people have expressed an urgent need to talk about the conflicts and difficult situations in their lives and have asked for my help.

I can't tell you how often I've heard frustrations like these:

> *My boss isn't fair.*
> *My employees take advantage.*
> *My next door neighbor is so inconsiderate.*
> *My coworker is driving me nuts.*
> *I feel like a pushover.*

And after telling me their stories, they invariably ask, *What can I do?*

Some of the stories I hear break my heart. I feel really bad for the people who seek me out, and at times I've even commiserated—I've been there myself. I think at one time or another we all have felt frustrated, tongue-tied, or fed up with someone else's behavior.

I listen with sympathy, but always there is a part of me that wants to reach out, give the person a shake, and say, "Why don't you do something about it?"

Over time, however, I made what I think is a significant discovery— *people don't say or do anything to the person bothering them mostly because they don't know what to say or do!*

I have also noticed a negative communication pattern in many of the comments I hear: when people have difficulty talking to someone in an appropriate manner about a situation that is bothering them, they simply don't talk with that person at all. Instead, they complain to anyone who will give them a sympathetic ear, including me. Some people come to my seminars just seeking an opportunity to vent their emotions.

And yet there are just as many people who, when faced with a bothersome situation, say or do something that, however well intentioned, makes the situation worse:

> *I told him that if he wanted a bloody nose . . .*
> *I said, "Who do you think you are, Miss High and Mighty!"*
> *I said, "Gee, I'm so sorry to have to bother you with this."*

I remember cringing as I listened to many of these stories. I thought, "There's got to be a better way!" Many people believed that they were doing or saying the right thing, yet it was often apparent to me, just hearing the stories, that they had not cleared things up with the other person. In fact in most cases, things had only gotten worse.

Lacking the skills to confront another person in a positive way, the people I met often ended up making their world less pleasant and more stressful, both for themselves and for the other people in it—whether they intended to or not.

I soon realized that there is a tremendous need for people to learn how to express themselves effectively in difficult situations. People need these skills to enable them to stand up for themselves. They need to learn how to confront positively instead of complaining or employing a host of other negative and self-destructive behaviors.

So I decided, once and for all, to meet that need.

This book is the result.

Mastering positive confrontation can improve your life. You will feel better about yourself. You will no longer behave like a wimp or a bully and will not be controlled by bad behaviors you may have adopted unintentionally along the way. You'll be able to deal with difficult people and situations directly and confidently. No more "I wish I had said . . . " or "If only I had thought to . . . " or "It's no big deal . . . " (when you know it is a big deal). Best of all, positive confrontation will often lead to a positive resolution—rather than to more conflict.

Over ten years ago the first edition of this book came out. Since that time I have continued to teach *The Power of Positive Confrontation* to people at all levels and from all types of organizations, including police officers in the Southwest, school board members in the Midwest, senior executives at a large utility in the Northeast, and over one thousand women at Microsoft's annual women's conference, two years in a row. These experiences have helped me fine-tune the ideas and the skills that are vital to positive confrontation, and what I learned has been added to this new edition.

The rise of social media has added convenient new ways for us to communicate and share our lives, as well as new ways for us to misunderstand and annoy each other. Now we have Twitter wars, friends unfriending one another, diners texting others at the table, employees quitting their jobs on YouTube, and so on. Therefore, a chapter addressing online conflict has been added to this edition. You will also find stories of conflicts people experience on Facebook, Twitter, Instagram, online groups, and blogs woven throughout the book.

I have received many emails and calls from people who read the first edition and want to share their experiences with positive confrontation, including the training director who called the book a "game changer." He only wished that he had read it years ago. It would have saved him a lot of unnecessary conflict.

I have heard that comment a lot.

Other comments include:

I don't feel frustrated anymore.
In the past I would have sulked or complained until the person got the hint, but now I can just say something.

Or

Annoying things don't bother me as much because I know I can say something now.

If you're like most of us, you were never taught the skills described in this book. They have already worked for thousands of people I have taught in my seminars, workshops, and coaching sessions. I believe they can work for you too.

PART I

Positive Confrontation:
What It Is and
How It Can Make
Your Life Better

Conflict, Conflict Everywhere

L ife is full of sticky situations, packed with difficult conversations, and
loaded with confrontation. How do you handle these situations, conversations, and confrontations? When someone's behavior is bothering
you—be it a relative, coworker, or neighbor—what do you say to that
person?

Maybe you don't say anything. If you don't, you're probably fed up,
worn-out, or just plain sick and tired of not being able to tell someone
who's close—or not so close—what's bothering you.

You are not alone if you feel this way.

Do you approach a problem with a friend or neighbor with good intentions but then lose it? Do you clam up, unfriend, storm out, or just
chicken out?

Do you feel walked on, annoyed, bothered, taken advantage of, frustrated, or upset by another person's behavior?

You guessed it! You are not alone if you have these feelings too. If you're
reading this book, you may be like the men and women from all types of
professions and all walks of life that I've taught or spoken with over the last
twenty years. These people feel the same way you do. They are tired of not
being able to tell someone when something is bothering them. They are
tired of avoiding difficult conversations, getting angry, or tolerating rude
behavior. No one sets out in life to become an unfriender, a door slammer,
or a big chicken. But people adopt these negative behaviors anyway, all the
time, and then they feel bad about themselves because of it.

Many people are honest enough with themselves to know they are not comfortable with confronting others. But they are stuck. What can they do about it?

Again, if you're like most of the people I've met and taught over the past twenty years, you probably could use some help in answering this question. These are smart, successful, well adjusted, and well liked people—and they don't know how to act either.

You may not be sure if you are having positive confrontations or not. Maybe you are simply curious about what positive confrontation means. What, you may be wondering, is the power that can be harnessed through it? How can it make your life better?

Are You Holding Yourself Back?

Whether or not you realize it, you may have a way of handling, or not handling, conflict that has been holding you back. From what? From getting ahead at work. From having more satisfying relationships with friends and loved ones. From feeling empowered in a world that can often leave you feeling powerless.

In this book you will learn how positive confrontation can improve your relationships, your self-esteem, your sense of well-being, and even your career. Positive confrontation can empower you in your relationships with others. If you adopt and practice the skills I talk about in this book, they *will* empower you in dealing with others. Though I can't make any promises or give you any guarantees, I can tell you this: I get emails, Facebook posts, comments on my blogs, phone calls, and people who come up to me after my seminars—and they all say the same thing. They tell me that my approach to handling confrontation works for them.

That is why I am certain it can work for you too.

The Big and Small Picture of Conflict

What exactly are the conflicts and the confrontations I'm addressing here? Let's consider the big picture of conflict first. The world isn't all bad, but our 24/7 news cycle with live Twitter updates can sometimes make you worry. There are wars. There are racial tensions, crimes, terrorists, politicians attacking each other, and schools running out of money. It's understandable that at times we feel drained of power or just drained.

Even our entertainment news is fraught with conflict. Every day we hear about celebrities engaging in Twitter wars and talk show hosts insulting their guests. Reality television often relies on conflict for ratings. When reality stars or contestants are rude, attack one other, fight in public, and generally behave badly, audiences tune in and ratings go up.

This book is *not* about global conflict or societal conflict. I can't help world leaders deal positively with conflict. I wish I could. I also can't make reality television stars get along. I can't make talk show hosts be polite to their guests. I can't stop Twitter wars. I wish I could do all of these things; believe me, the world would be a lot less stressful.

This book is about conflict on a smaller scale—the conflict, rudeness, and incivility you probably face in your life on a daily basis. It's about how we go through the day and interact with others, whether face-to-face interactions, texting, or tweeting.

Difficult Communication . . . Difficult Conversation

On a broader scale, heads of state have trouble talking to each other, getting their points across, being understood. This happens on the smaller scale too, with the person in the next cubicle, your roommate, your brother-in-law, your Facebook friend, or your bank teller.

Sometimes, in this smaller picture that is day-to-day living, we have a hard time talking to each other when there is conflict. We have a hard time expressing ourselves appropriately to others. We don't know what to say or how to say it. We don't know how other people will react if we tell them how we really feel. There are many other reasons why we feel uncomfortable having difficult conversations and dealing with conflict. Communicating successfully with others in uncomfortable situations is especially difficult. I will talk about why this is true in more detail in Chapter 3.

In this chapter I focus on the ability to communicate successfully. The effects of unsuccessful communication are obvious: road rage and airport rage; Facebook flameouts, cubicle clashes, roommate rumbles, and supermarket strife. Half the people you pass on a crowded street seem stressed out and in a hurry; the others are preoccupied or distracted by their phones. The presence of so much conflict and stress all around you can make you feel powerless. A silent frustration can take root that grows and keeps growing.

It's the Same Twelve Conflicts: Over and Over Again

During each seminar, I ask participants to describe on an index card a situation with another person that is bothering them. After conducting hundreds of seminars, I see the same conflicts over and over. These aren't the only conflict areas, but they are the most common.

Twelve Kinds of Behavior That Drive Us Nuts

1. **Space spongers.** They play their music too loud, even while wearing ear buds. They lurk around your work space, leave messes for others to clean up, or claim three tables in Starbucks as their new office space.
2. **Digitally distracted devils.** They can't have a face-to-face conversation without sending or receiving a text. This is the coworker who plays with his smartphone or iPad during meetings, and the friend who can't be in the moment because she's too busy making a video of it and posting it on Facebook.
3. **Bad borrowers.** They return your car with no gas, your favorite book with coffee stains, or take your stapler without asking. And money—it doesn't get paid back.
4. **Constant complainers.** Everyone knows one . . . the person who *always* has a problem or gripe that never gets resolved. You're tired of hearing about how your friend's mother-in-law makes catty comments or how unhappy your coworker is about the new boss.
5. **Interjecting interrupters.** Some people just can't let others have their say. They don't let you finish a sentence during a cocktail party or share your ideas during a meeting.

6. **Callous commentators.** This can be the neighbor who thinks your house needs to be painted, the friend who corrects your grammar, the person who posts racist or sexist jokes on Facebook, or your sister who, unsolicited, tells you she liked your hair better long.
7. **Work welchers.** Some people just don't do their fair share, whether it's the weekly chores, a group project for management, or a PTA volunteer committee.
8. **Request refusers.** These offenders don't respond to your emails, whether it's the data you need by Wednesday or the RSVP to the party you're hosting. Or you've asked your spouse to be on time for dinner and he is late again. Then there's the neighbor who lets her dog go in your yard despite the fact that you have put up a sign prohibiting it.
9. **Annoying askers.** Enough already! You're continually asked to sponsor your friend's many charitable causes, coordinate the bake sale, host your visiting relatives (plus their dogs), or take on extra work when you're swamped.
10. **Social media menaces.** These offenders share unflattering photos of you, tweet what they had for breakfast, chronicle their daily outrages, or flaunt their fantastic love lives/adorable children/ fabulous vacations/enviable accomplishments way too much on Facebook, Twitter, and Instagram.
11. **Holiday hasslers.** Who can relax? Your mother just doesn't understand that you need to go to your in-laws for Thanksgiving, or you want an adventure vacation in the woods but your significant other wants to lie in the sun on a tropical island. You love your family . . . but a week in the mountains with fifteen of them?
12. **Gruesome groomers.** You can smell her perfume and hear her bracelets jangling before you see her. He clips his fingernails in meetings. They floss at the dinner table. She wears her skirts way too short and he doesn't shower after his morning workout.

These twelve examples show how ordinary, routine interactions and relationship issues become problems. Too often conflicts that should be, and can be, easily resolved get messy, complicated, and frustrating. You end up in a confrontation that turns aggressive or you don't have a confrontation at all. The problem gets ignored.

Your coworker talks too loud and it's driving you crazy. A man steals your parking space on the street. Your sister-in-law makes a comment you find offensive. Your boss criticizes you but not your teammates: these may be run-of-the-mill communications problems, but they come up again and again for people everywhere, all the time. We ignore these behaviors, overlook them, or overreact for a simple reason: *we don't know what else to do.*

People think not having a confrontation is easier than having a confrontation. Not true. It's just that it's not easy to know what to say or how to say it, in a way that is both Polite and Powerful, if no one ever taught you.

I am talking about the ordinary conflicts that arise all the time, for everyone—at work, at home, standing in line at the bank, on Facebook, with your neighbors, your in-laws, or your kid's teacher. Difficult communication affects all areas of your life. I will use examples throughout this book that illustrate conflicts at work, at home, online, and just about everywhere else. The names and faces change. The details vary. All of the examples I cite in this book are real. I learned about them from participants in my workshops or they come directly from my own experience. I do protect people's privacy, but I don't make anything up. These examples prove, again and again, how badly people need the skills I talk about in this book.

The Communication Problem Is the Same

The unpleasant situations that I hear about may change, but the underlying communication problem is often the same: *we have a hard time talking to each other.* And if we can't talk to each other constructively about what's bothering us, we can't have positive confrontations and we can't resolve problems. The same is true for online conflict. Often the best way to resolve serious online conflict is to take the conversation offline. As I explain in Chapter 13, you may need to stop typing and talk to the person, and yet so many of us find this difficult to do, especially when we're not used to interacting with the person directly, either face-to-face or speaking by phone.

When we don't resolve conflicts, we don't feel good about the other person or ourselves. The effect can often be cumulative. It can sneak up on you, this feeling of powerlessness or anger. One difficult conversation you do not have leads to another you do not have. One difficult conversation that ends in shouting leads to another that ends in shouting. You feel taken advantage of, sick and tired, or mad. Or maybe you feel a little out of control. Feeling powerless or angry is not a fun or healthy way to go through life.

The problem we have with successfully resolving many kinds of day-to-day difficulties is the same and so is the solution—which you will learn about in this book. It will work for you if you have a hard time speaking up, or if you speak up too harshly, quickly, or aggressively. You can use this solution if you are sometimes too quick to respond with an angry email or a harsh Facebook post or tweet. In Parts II–III of this book, I present the solution as a series of communication skills and techniques that you can easily learn and adopt.

It's up to you to use the skills and techniques described in this book to positively resolve the conflicts in your life. I hope you will choose to make them a part of the way you operate out there in the world. You'll be glad if you do because these are life-enhancing skills that, in all likelihood, no one ever taught you. This isn't saying anything bad about you if you don't know them. Very few people ever learn how to have difficult conversations comfortably, since this is not taught in high school, college, or work orientation. Fewer of us go on to figure them out on our own.

What I Can't Help You With

In this book I am not going to teach you skills to deal with extreme or abusive situations. Sadly, a woman approached me after a seminar and asked me how she should handle her physically abusive husband. Though my heart went out to her, I told her positive confrontation was not a solution for her current situation. She needed professional help, and I urged her to get it.

I don't know what you should say if you meet someone on a dark street who makes you nervous. You should probably avoid a conversation and just get yourself to a safe place. While I do address how to deal with rude strangers, for the most part, I'm talking about those day-to-day conflicts that crop up, drive you crazy, and never seem to get better—not dangerous situations. As you will discover by the end of this book, addressing rude strangers may not be the necessity you thought it was when you started reading this book. You'll see.

How I Can Help You Solve the Problem of Not Being Able to Talk to People in Difficult Situations

I just told you what I can't do. Here is what I *can* do:

- Help you if you're having a hard time talking honestly to another person about something that's bothering you.
- Show you how to handle conflict better through Polite and Powerful behavior. You'll learn what it looks like, sounds like, and acts like.
- Improve your life in what will seem like a small way at first. Then the improvement will ripple. It will reach and spread, touching more and more corners of your life in a positive way.

"Oh, This Isn't for Me"

Oh, maybe it is. I don't care who you are, how much money you make or don't make. I don't care about your gender, your race, your religion, or what your hobbies are. Everyone, absolutely everyone, has conflict in life. At some point, you will eventually find yourself in a confrontation. The big question is, How will you handle it?

Many people think, believe, even insist that they're approaching conflict the right way. You may think you're an assertive person, but you may be wrong. Look at the following letter to Ann Landers. Though several years old, it describes the kind of story I hear all the time:

Dear Ann Landers: A few years ago I was in the elevator of a New York department store, and the woman in front of me kept swinging her head from side to side. Her hair hit me in the face every time. I finally tapped her on the shoulder and said, "The next time your hair hits me in the face, you will not need a haircut for a very long time . . . " Your readers might like to try my approach.

This woman believed that she was acting appropriately. She believed she was sticking up for herself, taking a stand, speaking up. But she blew it. She was not polite. She was rude. She was not powerful. She was aggressive. And to Ann Landers's credit, she didn't recommend this approach. I will give the woman who wrote this letter the benefit of the doubt. She probably had no idea she was behaving inappropriately. If I have learned anything over the last twenty years it is that people really do not know *how* they are behaving in difficult situations and confrontations. They do not understand how they appear to others and what effect their behavior can have on other people.

This is why, even if you think you would behave appropriately during a conflict, I challenge you to read this book. Then tell me if you're handling yourself and your difficult conversations in the best possible way.

It's Not Brain Surgery, But Brain Surgeons Need It Too

Okay, not everyone is so easily convinced that the power of positive confrontation is all that powerful. A man who attended one of my seminars sponsored by a professional association said, quite sarcastically, "Well, this sure isn't brain surgery."

"No, of course not," I said. "But that doesn't mean it can't change your life in a positive and lasting way." Then a surprising thing happened. A woman in the audience stood up and said, "I *am* a brain surgeon and I didn't know any of this. I've been frustrated because my supervisor has been asking me to work weekends all the time. He's not asking anyone else. I'm here because I keep saying to myself, 'I have to say something,' but I don't know what to say or how to say it."

Positive confrontation skills benefit everyone. Brain surgeons have trouble handling conflict on the job and at home. So do salespeople, homemakers, IT managers, administrative assistants, husbands, PTA presidents, Cub Scout leaders, wives, and significant others.

These skills are applicable to every area of your life. Anyone who has a problem telling coworkers, friends, family, and significant others their concerns—Politely and Powerfully—will benefit. It's also for anyone who has ever left a restaurant, movie theater, or grocery store thinking, "When that jerk butted ahead of me, I should have said, 'Hey, jerk! Whaddya think you're doing?'"

And this book is for anyone who thinks that telling a jerk off is a positive action. It's for anyone who may think that sticking up for yourself means putting another person down. As you'll soon discover, what we think is acceptable or appropriate behavior may actually be rude and unacceptable behavior.

So What Exactly Is Polite and Powerful Behavior?

Speaking of rude . . . Polite and Powerful *isn't*. Here's what it is:

It describes the way you handle yourself during a positive confrontation. It's more than saying please and thank-you.

It's more than having the guts to march up to someone and express yourself forcefully.

What Does Assertiveness Mean?

No one really knows. You can look it up in the dictionary. I ask people all the time to describe behavior that would be characterized as assertive. Usually what I hear is silence.

Ask ten people what it means to be assertive and you will get a shrug or you will get ten different answers. This is why "assertive" is not my favorite word for this kind of discussion. The woman who wrote to Ann Landers thought she was being assertive. People think of themselves as assertive; meanwhile, other people think of them as passive or aggressive. This is why "assertiveness" can get confusing. I call the behavior I talk about in this book Polite and Powerful because it's a more accurate description for the behavior used in a positive confrontation.

Polite and Powerful is a set of skills that combines what most people think of as *assertiveness* training with *etiquette* training. Twenty years ago, I began teaching both of these skill areas. More and more, I saw that many of the same issues I addressed in my assertiveness classes—becoming a powerful person—were cropping up in my etiquette classes—becoming a polite person—and vice versa. Many of the questions overlapped. Many of the skills overlapped. It was clear to me that the combination of Polite and Powerful behavior provided a practical skill area that many people need.

Minding More Than Your Manners

Business and social etiquette is more than learning about table manners, such as which water glass is yours at a business lunch or a wedding reception. In reality, that's only a small, small part of any modern etiquette training. (Your water glass, by the way, is on the right.)

Another critical but lesser known aspect of etiquette, whether in the board room or your living room, is understanding how to get along with others. Etiquette training teaches you how to make the best impression on others, including your boss, book group, customers, great-aunt, and neighbor.

Trust me when I tell you that a lot of people lacking etiquette skills don't get promoted—no matter how smart or technologically skillful they are. People with poor etiquette skills are not made president of their civic association. They are not asked to head important department projects or help out at the church bake sale, and then they grumble about it.

"Etiquette" is all about treating others the right way. The "right way" means with tact in both your words and actions. It is what you say and how you say it. It is treating people with kindness. This is the polite part of positive confrontation.

Etiquette Meets Assertiveness

In my seminars, I help people understand that they have a right to be heard and to speak up. But you have to act on this belief and you have to act correctly—that means Politely and Powerfully. Again, the combination of etiquette training and assertiveness training gets people to tune in to how they may be appearing to others. It helps them understand how their verbal and nonverbal communication skills are helping or harming an already difficult situation. We send silent messages out to others, all day long, day after day, often without knowing what messages we're actually sending.

Just being polite may not be enough to handle a difficult situation. You may come off as wimpy. If you are just powerful, that approach won't work either. Without the polite part, powerful behavior is often just aggression. You need both for positive confrontation.

I Had No Idea I Did That!

Once people tune in, many are in for a big surprise! Oh, I could tell you stories that you would find outrageous. Things you would think no one would do. But the fact is, people do unbelievable things every day. I know of a high-level executive who licked his knife at an important business lunch and lost thirty million dollars' worth of business as a result. Or a woman at a conference in New Orleans who posted, "Off to another stupid meeting. Would much rather be on Bourbon Street." You might not do anything so outrageous, but we all have bad habits.

When a client of mine complained about his "unfair" boss, I suggested that he film himself giving a presentation. He was shocked to discover that literally every other word out of his mouth was "okay." He heard how bad he sounded. No wonder he wasn't asked to give more of the department's key presentations. *Before* he watched the video, he thought his boss "had it out for him" by not giving him the plum assignments. *After* viewing himself, he understood that he was probably holding himself back.

Like this man, you'll learn how to identify and break habits that have been undermining your success at work and satisfaction in your relationships. You will learn about the specific dos and don'ts of positive confrontation using verbal and nonverbal communication skills and techniques. And you'll learn about the benefits of positive confrontation throughout this book.

The Benefits of Positive Confrontation

Speaking of the benefits of positive confrontation . . . there are many. But explaining the benefits—the increased self-esteem and lower stress level for starters—experienced by Polite and Powerful people is a little like explaining the benefits of exercise. You know why it is good for you but may not know how to go about getting started. I'm not just saying that Polite and Powerful can change your life in a positive and lasting way. I can prove it. I can prove it in the way I handle myself in tough situations. My filing cabinets and my email inbox are filled with positive testimonials I have received from participants at my seminars.

People describe to me the relief they feel when they finally confront someone about something that may have been bothering them for a while. Others say that they no longer feel taken advantage of by people at work or that they are able to quickly resolve misunderstandings with friends. As a result, people feel happier at work and in their personal lives. Most of the time, you will feel the benefits in little ways—an improved relationship with an in-law or coworker here or a less stressful day at work there. But the little ways will start to add up and then you will find that you are less stressed and feel more in control.

The benefits of positive confrontation can change your life. Learning how to be Polite and Powerful will not cure all of your problems, but if you are unable to tell other people how their behavior is affecting you or you are speaking up but still not getting resolution, this book can help you.

Trust me on this too: it's much better to be an ex-wimp than an active wimp. When you practice Polite and Powerful behavior, you can be a positive role model and a true leader rather than someone who intimidates employees. You will discover creative space in your brain you didn't know you had. And you didn't know you had it because complaining, or a host of other nonpositive behaviors, was sucking up that creative energy. Not being Polite and Powerful can wear you out mentally and drain you physically. Two more reasons—enhanced emotional well-being and better health—to give positive confrontation a try.

Where Do We Go from Here?

After a brief confession from me, an exploration into who you are as a confronter and how you got the way you are, we head right into the land of positive confrontation. Step by step and brick by brick, we will build the skills you need so that you too can become a Polite and Powerful person. I have seen it proven time and time again—when people have the right skills and the right tools, an approach rooted in being Polite and Powerful works.

With practice, it's surprisingly easy to learn and apply the skills of Polite and Powerful behavior that will lead you to positive confrontation. I've created a simple model called WAC'em, which you'll learn about in much greater detail soon. WAC'em will help you overcome what is often the biggest obstacle to confrontation—figuring out exactly what's bothering you and what you want to say to (or ask for from) the other person—all in a way that's positive. Putting your words together for a difficult conversation or confrontation won't be a problem anymore.

This sounds like a cinch. And in time, it will become easy for you. But in the beginning you will see that putting Polite and Powerful into action can be tricky. The process of figuring out what's really bothering you and what you really want from the other person can be challenging. Though it requires some effort at first, WAC'em will help you prepare for confrontations and difficult conversations in a step-by-step, brick-by-brick manner. Later, handling the sticky situations and having the conversations that now make you wince will become much simpler. You'll see.

Along the road, I will encourage you to do four things:

1. Gain awareness of how you handle yourself, including your confrontational style.
2. Limit the assumptions you make about the behavior of other people.
3. Have a confrontation when necessary—and be Polite and Powerful when you do.
4. Learn how to reduce the amount of conflict in your life.

Avoiding Conflict

Are you surprised by number 4 above? Isn't the point of this book to have positive confrontations? Yes—when it's necessary and appropriate. But Polite and Powerful people know how to present themselves in a way that invites less conflict. Also, Polite and Powerful people learn when "letting something go" is the better, healthier alternative than engaging in a confrontation.

Practice, Practice, Practice

Learning new skills takes time. You will have to practice. I don't want you to put this book down and go tell your boss you don't think he's fair or your best friend that she's bossy. Start slowly. Build your confidence. In time, you will have a whole new way of operating in the world, a way that's more effective and positive. Over time, Polite and Powerful behavior will come naturally to you. You'll feel better about yourself. You'll feel better about your relationships with other people. You may not always get what you want from the other person, but I promise you that if you practice and work at having positive confrontations you will at least know where you actually stand with the other person. And you can be certain that you'll be the one standing tall.

For now, feel good knowing that you're on your way.

2

The Confrontational Road Less Traveled
Is Paved by Bullies and Wimps

A s I told you in Chapter 1, I've met more people than I can count who have a hard time resolving day-to-day conflicts positively. But my knowledge of this communication problem doesn't come simply from teaching Polite and Powerful skills to others. My knowledge is also firsthand. At one time in my life, there was no one in the world who needed this book more than I did.

This leads me to a confession: I used to be a wimp. A big one. I'm not kidding—huge.

This surprises most of the people who attend my seminars about how to confront people in a positive way.

Think about it. How else would I know this subject so well? How else could I be so enthusiastic about this communication issue?

Back to the huge wimp. The professionals I teach look at me and say, "You! No way. You don't look like a wimp." It's true, I don't. I'm tall and I stand tall. I talk to huge crowds and look at ease. I have command of my words and of my gestures. I can walk across a stage without feeling like I might fall or faint. And after years of teaching hundreds of seminars, you can bet my voice reaches the last row of just about any room.

Yet there I was. Queen of the wimps.

Once Upon a Time . . .

When I was a kid, I was incredibly shy. Being tall wasn't the greatest feature to have then. Now I love it, but then . . . there I was, feeling like a skinny tree, all elbows and knees. It was the era of "children should be seen and not heard," and I think that was especially true for little girls of my generation. We were encouraged to play nicely and be ladies—as we still often tell little girls. Societal gender norms do not change quickly. A woman told me that the coach of her daughter's basketball team told the players during a game to get out there and "play like ladies." How, her daughter wanted to know, was she supposed shoot baskets and be a lady?

Little boys got—and still get—messages about how to behave in confrontations. Many boys are encouraged to be tough: "Don't get mad, get even." Of course, when I was growing up, crying for most boys was out of the question, and after they enter middle school nowadays, it often still is. Tears mean "he's a wimp."

Kids get messages from their parents about how to handle conflict and other people. You went to school, church, Little League, Girl Scouts . . . and you got messages there too, messages about how you were expected to behave. Many of those messages were good, but because we lacked positive role models for handling conflict, some of them may not have been so helpful: *It's okay to yell when you're unhappy. Just ignore someone's bad behavior. It's okay not to talk to people if you're upset with them.*

Childhood Messages Can Chase You into Adulthood

Again, some of these messages were good, but others may be causing you problems to this day. Messages about how to handle difficult situations don't just get in, they stay in. Over time, your self-confidence is chipped away, or you have trouble communicating in relationships, or it's easier to get new friends than deal with the old ones. For me, it was classic wimp syndrome: I fantasized about speaking up, but I couldn't bring myself to do it.

Naturally, being a wimp followed me out of adolescence and into the adult world. What better place to discover exactly the width and depth of your wimpiness than in your professional life? Many years ago, when I was first starting out in the corporate world, I worked for a largely male-dominated aerospace company. I can tell you tales of how I was slighted or treated rudely by people at work, everyone from a big boss to the woman in the parking lot who screamed at me for taking what she considered "her spot." But I'm not going to tell them all, just one. The one that changed everything for me:

Once during a meeting with one of the company's directors, he told me, "Why don't you stay home and have babies like a good gal."

Well!

Lucky for me I had the good luck of working for a director named Ann Davis. She was one of two high-level women in the entire company. She was confident and self-assured—two things I wasn't then. She became my mentor. So after the director said these demeaning words to me I ran, top speed, into Ann's office, crying of course.

She asked me, "Why didn't you just tell him you were offended by his comment?"

"You mean I can tell him that?" I asked.

I look back now and think, "Duh, Barbara!" But then I honestly didn't know that I had a right to do this until Ann told me that I did. What I did instead of telling that director he offended me was complain. And did I ever complain! I complained to Ann and my sisters and my neighbor . . . that was my standard operating procedure. If someone treated me unfairly, poorly, or rudely, I used to complain to my girlfriends about that person's behavior. I'd complain to my hairdresser or the stranger sitting next to me on the plane. I wasn't picky. I just needed an ear. I could talk for hours and hours about it. I could wear your ear out and still want to complain more.

But I never said a word to the person bugging me. Never. Not one word. And by not confronting, I felt bad about myself.

Speaking of Crummy Self-Esteem

Let's get it over with—the self-esteem part of any discussion about confronting others. Here's what I have learned about self-esteem: we can all suffer from bad self-esteem at times, some of us more than others. Yes, it feels bad.

Yes, it probably holds us back at times. I certainly recognize that it's a reason why many of us don't confront positively. But it's not the *only* reason.

The preoccupation with low self-esteem is not necessarily helpful to this discussion. As I was trying to cure my own wimpiness, I read books. They helped to a degree, but I found many of them frustrating. Mostly these books talked to me about why I had gotten the wimpy way that I was—poor self-esteem. I knew that I had poor self-esteem. I wasn't a complete wimp, or hopeless in every situation in my life, but, yes, I needed help with my self-esteem. Why else was I reading the book in the first place? I wasn't looking for someone to psychoanalyze me. I was looking for a step-by-step guide on how to assert myself positively.

There was no guide. But slowly over time, with patience and practice, I did learn how to confront others in a more positive way and my self-esteem improved dramatically. I looked to Ann, my mentor, for continued guidance. Sometimes just watching her in action was inspiration. I saw how she remained calm, no matter what the other person said or did. In tense situations, her body language was strong but not overwhelming. Her word choice always seemed Polite yet Powerful.

I realized that in order to fulfill my career goals, I was going to have to become a Polite and Powerful person too. I understood the cost of not being one. When I was a photojournalist, I once applied for an editor's job. I was told that I would be contacted for an interview. They forgot to interview me. At the time, I accepted that.

I let them forget me!

A New Formula for Success

I knew that I would never get anywhere if I continued to let people forget to interview me. I was going to have to lose my fear of sticking up for myself. And I was going to have to do this without alienating other people. I don't care what your gender is, what era you're living in, or what technical skills or special talents you may have. You cannot just assert yourself any way you want and automatically have people respect you. You have to deal with other people—even people who are bugging you—in a respectful manner. We are now living in a world where the wrong tweet or blog post can get you fired. You may not mean to be offensive or act inappropriately, but if you want to rise to the top of your profession, start your own business, or run your neighborhood association, you must learn how to get along with other people.

I'm sure you know someone who is highly successful but not well liked, perhaps the hot-tempered CEO of your company whose very presence causes people to freeze in fear at what he may say or do. In my opinion, this is just the powerful without the polite and he may even be a bit of a bully. I don't care how successful this person may be in business. To me, respect carved out of fear means you're not a successful person in your relationships or in life in general. I believe that you can be both Polite *and* Powerful and still have people like and respect you. I believe that having good relationships with others is the more positive way to go through life. Otherwise, I don't think success is worth it. I would never want to be the kind of person who enters a room and instills fear in others. Respect—yes. Fear—no.

Back in my wimpy days, my goal might not have been becoming the CEO of a Fortune 500 company, but still, I had career goals that were important to me. I had a lot to learn, and I did learn. With Ann's coaching, I was able to tell the director I worked with that I didn't like his comments about a woman's duty to stay at home and be a "good gal." The next time around for an editor's job, I made sure I was interviewed.

As my confrontations became more positive, I started having some positive outcomes.

Once when I brought it to a manager's attention that he kept cutting me off in meetings, he apologized and listened to me in the future. Eventually he liked my ideas and he promoted me.

Speaking of Good Self-Esteem . . .

I started feeling better about myself because I liked the way I handled myself. I started handling myself better in my relationships. This was important change for me. I was a single mom with a son. I wanted to set a good example for my son on how to handle himself in life's sticky situations. Kids can tell a hypocrite from a mile off. You have to live what you preach.

I didn't want to end up in another relationship like my first marriage, where I had a hard time expressing my true and honest feelings.

I also didn't want to stew over what I perceived as slights anymore. Like the time my cousin came to visit me for the weekend. As soon as she came to my house, she said, "Yuck! You got another dog. He's so big and ugly!"

Well, I'm a dog person. My dog is a well loved member of my family. I was offended by my cousin's comment about him and I wanted to say something to her. But what? I was stuck. I'm sure you know how that feels. You're indignant and tongue-tied at the same time. It's very frustrating. At first I didn't say anything. I needed to get my thoughts together. Later, though, I realized I couldn't, and didn't want to, let her comment go without speaking up. It was affecting my ability to enjoy her visit. So I finally got my guts up and confronted her. She couldn't have apologized faster and we had a great time after that.

The old wimpy me would have held my silent grudge. That grudge would have festered. After she left I would have set fire to the carpet running to the telephone. I would have been complaining to my sisters and friends about what a jerk she was before her car was off my block. But because I had spoken up, I was free of this behavior. Wow, did that feel good.

In smaller ways and then bigger ways, my life got better. My stress level went down as my confidence went up. So when I tell you that the skills you'll learn in this book will help you resolve conflicts and have those difficult conversations, I know this firsthand. I know firsthand how much better it feels being Polite and Powerful. It's a new kind of freedom.

I want you to be free too.

Looking Back Now

If I had known how to confront positively years ago, it would have helped me in my first marriage—by ending it sooner, because ending it was for the best. I'm certain it would have helped during my divorce. (Talk about difficult conversations!) It would have helped me deal with rude people in the grocery store or a college professor who gave me a hard time.

Polite and Powerful provides you with tools for all areas of your life. It would have helped me reduce the overall level of stress in my life. You'll learn, as I have, how to look at your behavior to discover if you may be a source of conflict for someone else.

What Messages Did You Get?

Remember the messages I received to be "a good gal"? You received messages too. Take a few minutes and think about what they were. Think of how these messages may continue to influence your interactions with others, especially in difficult situations. You may want to write these messages down so that you can reflect on them and understand how they may still be influencing you. You may also want to try listing all the ways your life would improve if you stopped letting these old messages dictate how you handle conflict now.

The next chapter will help you identify the confrontational style you have, most likely, unknowingly adopted. Understanding who you are as a confronter is the first step in saying, "I don't want to yell at people anymore," "I'm tired of ignoring problems," or "I want to handle myself better."

You don't have to let old messages influence you anymore. You can break free. You have already started.

3

Confronters: The Bully, the Wimp, the Big Mouth in Action

You already know who I was as a confronter—a wimp. Now it's time for you to ask yourself, "Who am I as a confronter?" Who are you when you're dealing with coworkers, family members, and friends in sticky situations?

You can't say you don't know who you are as a confronter or that you're no particular kind of confronter. You *are* someone as a confronter. Everyone is.

I know this is hard. No one wants to admit, "I scream my head off in confrontations," or "I avoid difficult conversations like the plague." Admitting to these behaviors is admitting to others that your behavior is unattractive or self-defeating. I hated to think of myself as a wimp.

But if you avoid people during difficult situations, yell at them or employ other kinds of destructive behaviors, it means you've fallen into a negative confrontational pattern. More people than you could ever count, right this minute, everywhere in the world, in offices and homes, on Twitter and Facebook, are having negative confrontations. No one wants to be the bully or the wimp, yet it's a pattern we've fallen into. It's human nature to keep doing what we do. This is true even for the negative things that we wish we could stop doing. Even when we realize our behavior is bad, negative, or driving the people around us crazy, unless we have a better behavior to replace it with, we continue to act in ways that have a negative impact on ourselves and others.

So, Who Are You?

Most people don't know who they are as a confronter. You probably haven't given it much thought before. Start thinking about it now. Try to remember the last confrontation you had with a friend or coworker. How did it go? Did you raise your voice? Did you give him the silent treatment instead of speaking up? Did you cry or pound your fist? Did you get your point across? Were you able to be honest about how you really felt? Did you give her a chance to speak honestly to you? Did you unfriend her without being honest about why?

Being honest during a confrontation can be extremely difficult. There are many reasons why we hold back from telling another person the truth about how we feel. We worry that we'll hurt his feelings. We worry that she won't like us anymore. There are additional reasons why we hold back or lose our tempers during confrontations. We'll explore these reasons in more detail shortly.

As you read through this chapter, I want you to remember that no matter what behavior you've been employing in confrontations, you can be honest *and* you can choose your words carefully. You *can* treat the other person with respect. You *can* handle your body language in a way that makes you look powerful—if you know the skills to enable you to do so.

But what if you don't know these skills?

Then, of course, handling yourself well is going to be harder, if not impossible.

Often we don't handle ourselves well. This is why instead of having the conversation with the person who is bugging you, you do or say nothing, or you do or say something you regret.

The last time you wanted to tell somebody something honestly and didn't open your mouth, did you think, "It's no big deal?" or "Maybe next time?" or "He's just a jerk?"

Maybe it wasn't a big deal. Maybe there will be a next time. Maybe the guy was a jerk. Maybe. Maybe not. Yet another benefit to understanding the art of positive confrontation is that it can enable you to think "it's no big deal" and actually mean it. With practice and patience, you'll get there. I promise you can. If the Queen of the Wimps—me—can get there, you can too. For now, concentrate on being honest with yourself about your confrontational style. If you're ignoring a friend or relative's bothersome behavior and saying to yourself "it's no big deal" when in your heart, deep down, you know it matters to you, then you've got a problem. If you are yelling your head off during meetings and saying to yourself "I wish I hadn't done that *again*," you have a problem there too.

"I'll Get 'Em Next Time!"

When you were confronted by another person's bothersome behavior and you found yourself freezing up instead of speaking up, were you full of regret? Did you say to yourself, "I'll say something next time?"

Is there a next time?

Probably not.

Or if you lost your cool with the person, did you think, "The next time, I'll handle myself better." Did you handle yourself better the next time?

Probably not.

Usually you won't say something the next time or be calm the next time unless you change what you've been doing. And if making that change has been hard for you, you're not alone. A lot of people make vows about how they will behave during the next sticky situation or the next difficult conversation. But aren't you tired of making vows that you break? You get all pumped up with confidence and excitement and then you open your mouth and nothing comes out or the wrong thing comes out.

Welcome to the planet of the wimps and bullies.

Before You Can Be Honest with Others . . .

It isn't always easy being honest with others and it isn't always easy being honest with yourself. Developing self-awareness, however, depends on your willingness to be honest with yourself. It's often not fun. Especially in the beginning, when you're uncovering your behavioral blunders, it can seem downright unpleasant. Yes, it's tempting to ignore the glitches in your otherwise not so bad behavior. It's tempting to say to yourself, "I have friends. People like me. I'm doing fine."

Yes, I'm sure people like you and you have friends and much of your life is good. You probably are an honest person in other areas of your life, but that doesn't mean your confrontational style is a positive and honest one. It is essential that you figure out who you are as a confronter. You need to become more aware of what pattern of behavior you may have. You need to discover if you're honest with others or not. Only then can you can modify, improve, and, if necessary, get a whole new confrontational style. This process of self-discovery is worth it because your life and your relationships can get better than they are now. Positive confrontation will improve your life in so many ways.

Self-Assessment Quizzes Can Help

I used to feel bad after taking self-assessment quizzes, as I suddenly had a whole new problem to worry about. Then I realized that the only way to change is to start with self-knowledge. Change is not really possible without it. So, even if you're tempted to skip over this part, please don't. Take this short quiz. It's important!

When Interacting with Others

As I'm sure you've figured out by now, if you answered "true" to even a few of these questions, you've fallen into a negative confronting pattern. If you answered "not sure," chances are you may have a negative confronting pattern.

If you can't answer these questions definitively, your awareness of your own behavior is something you need to work on. For a few days, pay attention to how you handle conflict at work, in a line, at the movies, or on your Facebook page. Do you address someone else's rude or annoying behavior? If so, what do you say or post? If you ignored someone else's bothersome behavior, do you know why? Paying attention to these kinds of things will help you develop an awareness of your confrontational style.

When Interacting with Others

	TRUE	FALSE	NOT SURE
1. I ignore other people's behavior even if it bothers me.	●	○	○
2. I tell other people about someone's behavior and its effect on me without talking about it directly with that person.	●	○	○
3. I will often say "I'm sorry" to things that aren't my fault.	○	●	○
4. If I have a problem with a friend, I will stop calling or texting him until he gets the hint that I'm upset.	○	●	○
5. I believe that other people are usually the cause of the problem.	●	○	○
6. I can't help it; I yell when I'm upset.	○	●	○
7. I have said to myself, "She should know that it's not okay to say or do that to me."	●	○	○
8. It is important that I always win or get my way.	○	●	○
9. I have slammed doors, pounded my fist, or or thrown things when upset.	○	●	○
10. I worry that if I tell people what's bothering me, their feelings will be hurt or they won't like me anymore.	○	●	○
11. I think there are a lot of rude, insensitive, and selfish people out there in the world.	●	○	○
12. If I confront someone, I will make it seem like it's my fault so that I won't hurt her feelings.	○	●	○

What Holds You Back from Confronting?

As you develop an awareness of your confrontational style, be aware also of the most common reasons why people don't confront. These five reasons crop up again and again. Read on to discover if you see yourself in any of these patterns.

Five Reasons Why You May Not Be Confronting

Here are the most common reasons I've discovered why people aren't confronting others:

1. You think, "The other person *must* know that his behavior is inappropriate or bothersome." There is no jar deep enough to hold all of the nickels I get for this one: "Shouldn't he already know that what he is doing is upsetting to me?" or "How come I have to tell her? She should know that's rude." Well, guess what? People don't always know.

This story may be hard to believe, especially if you're a woman, but about a year ago, a man in one of my classes was horrified to discover how much the women he worked with resented being called "hon." His father and grandfather always said it and it became his habit too. He thought he was being friendly.

People make very quick assumptions, usually negative ones, about the motivations of others. Usually too quick and too negative. What you think is inappropriate may be fine for the other person. And what's acceptable or common knowledge for one person may not be for another. Like Kate's boss. He would criticize her but never compliment her. She said to me, "Why do I have to say anything to him? Why do I have to ask for good feedback? He should know this."

I said, "Maybe he doesn't know. Maybe he thinks it's only appropriate to talk to you when there's a problem."

This works in the opposite direction too. A supervisor has difficulty telling employees what they are doing is wrong. He thinks, "They should know why I'm upset with them." But why should they? People can't read other people's minds.

I met a woman with two younger sisters. Their parents had been hurt in an accident and required constant help. She was handling all the details of their care. She resented it. Finally, after stewing for several weeks, she confronted her sisters. "Why aren't you helping me?" she demanded. "It's not fair."

Her sisters were shocked. "We thought you wanted to be the one to handle it and be in charge. You always have in the past. You're the big sister."

They were only too happy to help.

Here's another story. Two colleagues were upset at their college interns for taking long lunches and assumed the interns were abusing the system. One of the men had to cut his own lunch short to have telephone coverage at his office because he knew his intern would not be back when she was supposed to be. After my seminar, they decided to confront them. The two coworkers met beforehand and figured out what to say to the interns. When they finally said something, they discovered that the interns didn't know about the lunch schedule. No one ever told them.

2. I don't want to hurt the other person's feelings. This one holds people back from confronting people they know well, acquaintances, and even people they don't know. You wouldn't believe the number of people who tell me they can't get off the phone with telemarketers. It's not because they want the product; it's because they have a hard time saying no.

With people we do know, we want to preserve the relationship at all costs. We worry that saying something will jeopardize the relationship.

"If you don't have anything nice to say, don't say anything at all." Just about everyone grows up with this advice. It's bad advice. Don't misunderstand. I teach business etiquette. I would never tell you to be rude, but are you always going to say nice things? Of course not! The Polite and Powerful spin to this saying is: "Say what you mean, mean what you say, but don't say it meanly."

Engaging in confrontation seems to go against the nurturing role to which so many women have been conditioned. Many women are raised to be the peacemakers. If you're a woman who has ever said to a friend, "Are you mad at me?" or "Don't be mad at me," you may have been conditioned this way too.

This is an issue for men too. Santiago is an attorney who likes his secretary as a person, but he doesn't like the mistakes she makes on his documents. He admitted to me that he was afraid that if he confronted her about her mistakes, he would hurt her feelings and she would start to cry. Maybe she would cry and get upset with him if he said something. But what are the consequences of his silence? He admitted that he was "cool to her" when she made mistakes. Is that better? I don't think so. I encouraged him to be honest with his secretary. Maybe she would improve her performance and become a better proofreader.

3. You mean I'm allowed to tell people I don't like their behavior? Some people don't know they have this right. This was me many years ago. I didn't understand that I could tell someone my concerns about his or her bothersome behavior or annoying comments. I hear it all the time now: "Can I really tell her I don't like it when she does that?"

"Yes," I say. "Yes, yes, yes."

Brittany won't tell her boss that another colleague got recognition for a job they both worked on. "He's the boss," she said. "It's not my place to tell him about this."

But it is her place. As I pointed out, who else is going to give her the recognition?

Jack has this problem too. A friend of his has been driving him crazy. "He wants me to join an incentive sales program. I don't want to join. He keeps asking and I keep saying no."

I said to Jack, "Why don't you tell him that you'd like him to stop asking."

"Oh," Jack said. "I guess I never thought about it."

"Well," I told him, "think about it now."

A woman told me that she's tired of her aunt calling her with unsolicited opinions. "You mean it's okay to tell her I don't always want to hear her opinion?" Yes, I told this woman, if you do it Politely and Powerfully—absolutely.

4. I'm afraid of what might happen. Again, being honest involves risks. Even if you have a positive confrontation and are able to be honest, that doesn't guarantee you will like the outcome. Depending on the nature of the relationship, the confrontation could be seen as a power struggle.

You may not have power or leverage, and you may not get what you're asking for.

This risk often occurs in work-related relationships. If your conflict is with someone higher up in the food chain, what will be the consequences of having a confrontation? You could confront your boss on something, but it is your boss, so sometimes, no matter what, it will be his or her way. Because you're the underling, the higher-up may not appreciate or want your honesty. Could you lose your job even if you handle yourself Politely and Powerfully? Though I can tell you it doesn't happen a lot, it does happen. Your boss may hold your honesty against you. Just because she says, "I really want to know what you think," doesn't mean she really wants to know. In Chapter 9, I'll talk more about how to weigh the risk versus the possible gains of confronting someone higher up than you are. For now, understand that yes, there can be risks associated with being honest with your boss.

There can be risks in personal relationships too. You may worry that confronting a friend or loved one will upset that person and negatively impact the relationship.

Here's a story I've heard a few times in one form or another. An unhappy man goes to his neighbor's leasing agent or landlord about a problem with his neighbor instead of to the man directly. I asked him why. He said, "I'm concerned about how he'll react."

Meanwhile the neighbor in question is wondering why his neighbor didn't come to him and talk about his problem. I don't blame the neighbor. He may not have known he was bugging his neighbor. Why not give him the benefit of the doubt?

And then there are strangers. Maybe it's smart to be afraid of what might happen if you confront a stranger. Since you don't know the person, you don't know how he may respond. This keeps people from speaking up. I tell people, "Use your judgment," but often because they're afraid of the reaction they will get, they don't say anything when they should.

A woman's company was flying her into town so she could attend my seminar. She told me she didn't want to tell the man next to her on the plane that she could hear his music even though he was wearing ear buds. "Why?" I asked.

"I didn't know him," she said. "I didn't know how he'd react."

How would he react? On the plane? With all those people around? Nine times out of ten, the person turns the music down. She could have spoken up.

She was in the right seminar.

5. I'm afraid of becoming aggressive. People think that if they get upset or angry they will automatically explode, so they deny that they're upset and they don't confront.

People confuse anger and aggression. They are *not* the same. Anger is the emotion. Aggression is the behavior. Emotions aren't good or bad. It's what you do or don't do as a result of feeling them that can be good or bad. You can learn to express your anger Politely and Powerfully.

Tamica can't confront her employee after she's discussed inappropriate subjects—more than once—during their department meeting. "I'm afraid I'm going to start yelling and have a hard time stopping," she said. But what if Tamica keeps holding back? She's bound to explode sooner or later and then what will be the consequences to her relationship with the employee? The relationship will probably suffer.

A father who won't confront his son about coming home late at night has the same problem. He won't speak up because he doesn't trust himself to keep his temper in check if his son talks back. He's tired of fighting with him. But strong feelings don't just go away. Chances are he'll blow up one day anyhow. Wouldn't it be better if he could have a calm conversation with his son before that happens? I think so!

Three Nonconfronters in Action

You may not confront because of one of the reasons above, but you actually do something. To give you an idea of what you may be doing when you're not confronting, I've profiled three common types of nonconfronters in terms of their behavior.

The Complainer

Our first nonconfronter is a complainer. Complainer is a nice way of saying "wimp." As you already know, this used to be me.

This person doesn't confront the one who is saying or doing something bothersome. She needs to complain in order to get relief from her bad feelings. And does this person complain? Freely. To friends, families, coworkers, anyone who will listen. Unfortunately, the relief a complainer feels is often short-lived.

Alyssa's manager makes fun of her in front of other people. She won't say anything to him, but goes home and cries on the telephone with her sister. Then her husband gets home and she talks about it for the rest of the night. Does this stop her manager from making fun of her? No. He doesn't know how she feels, so he's not going to stop.

A man complains to his wife about his friend who stands him up—again—at the racquetball court. But does he tell his friend. No!

Complainers waste an enormous amount of energy.

The Avoider

Avoiders waste creative energy too. They are wimps who will do just about anything to avoid confronting people who may be bothering them. They say, "It's not that big of an issue," when it is an issue. "Why rock the boat?" Often they don't just avoid having a confrontation; they avoid the other person too. It's easier than hurting someone's feelings.

Beth used to take a morning walk with her neighbor. But the neighbor was constantly complaining about her husband, boss, noise pollution, and how she couldn't get decent oranges at the produce stand. You name it—she complained about it.

Beth didn't want to hear such negative talk. This was her only time of day to relax. She told me she didn't want to hurt her neighbor's feelings so she just found excuses not to walk with her. It didn't occur to Beth that the excuses were obvious and that the neighbor's feelings were probably hurt anyway.

This woman was an avoider. Instead of being direct and honest, avoiders make up excuses and love to leave voice mails or send text message regrets: "OMG my car got towed . . . sorry, can't make it."

The woman who told me this story is an avoider too: "A relative who lives with me watches how I do things, like fixing a sandwich, and tells me how she does it, implying that I am doing it incorrectly. It really upsets me, but I don't want to hurt her feelings. I find myself sneaking into the kitchen to avoid her comments."

How can it not bother you to have your every move watched? People shouldn't have to sneak around in their own houses.

A manager in the financial services industry revealed that his counterpart "calls me to brag about her new deal. She goes on and on. I'm happy for her and I don't want to hurt her feelings by saying something, but it really wastes my time. I always let her calls go to voice mail."

I encouraged him to stop avoiding her and start talking to her—Politely and Powerfully.

A pharmaceutical sales rep got angry with one of his doctors who said he was prescribing his drugs, and even though the rep knew this wasn't true, he could not confront him. He kept saying, "Next time, I'll say something." But he couldn't bring himself to do it. Unfortunately he couldn't let his negative feelings go. He just stopped calling on the doctor. As a result, he and his company lost business. This kind of behavior is not going to advance anyone's professional image or career.

Even people in positions of authority can be secret avoiders. A CEO of a utility company admitted that at the end of the day he would cut through a conference room in order to avoid an overzealous director who was always stopping him and asking him complicated questions in the hallway.

However, the ultimate avoider is the woman in one of my overseas seminars who said, "I don't confront my friends; I just keep getting new ones."

The Pretender

Denial. Denial. Denial. Pretenders accept things, which if they were being honest, they wouldn't. "There is no problem, none whatsoever; things couldn't be better." Unlike avoiders, pretenders can't even admit they have difficult feelings. Sadly, these are also people whose health suffers, often chronically. I met a woman who was "encouraged" by upper management to take an overseas assignment with the international division of her company. She didn't want to leave the United States but couldn't admit that because she was afraid it would hurt her career. She told everyone, even herself, that she had no problem with it—until her hair started falling out. Her doctor told her it was stress. She finally had to speak to her boss because when your hair is falling out of your head, it gives you incentive to stop pretending.

Parents I know will not confront their son about his disruptive behavior. He smokes cigarettes, cuts class, and hangs out with a kid who has an arrest record. They say he's going through a phase. Maybe they don't want to deal with his real problems. Whatever their reasons for not speaking up, pretending that problems don't exist doesn't make them go away. Often they get worse and worse over time. I wonder what will happen to this boy in the future. Is he headed for bigger trouble? Unless his parents can stop pretending his behavior is acceptable, he may be.

The Price Nonconfronters Pay

Complainers, avoiders, and pretenders have other things in common besides their wimpiness. They have high stress levels, low self-esteem, and often don't get a favorable resolution to the issue. What about the person's bothersome behavior causing the stress? It continues, of course. Why should it stop? These nonconfronters can complain, avoid, and pretend all they like, except their problems with others don't evaporate. This form of behavior lends itself to feelings of powerlessness. What a crummy way to go through life!

People Who Do Confront—But Incorrectly

Then there are the people who do confront, but not Politely and Powerfully. They often are bewildered by the negative outcome and/or end up feeling even worse. There are three common reasons why this can happen during a confrontation:

Three Reasons Why Confrontations Can Become Negative

1. You repress your feelings and then blow up. Feelings don't go away. Ariama took a continuing education class. She liked the woman who sat next to her—until she became an annoying gum snapper. Finally Ariama couldn't take it anymore and blew up: "Don't you know how *bleep, bleep* annoying that is?" The snapper was embarrassed and immediately stopped, but in the future she sat far away from Ariama.

What would have happened if Ariama had approached the gum snapper in a Polite and Powerful fashion? Maybe they would still sit next to each other.

When Ariama yelled at the gum snapper she learned—the hard way—that feelings stay inside you. They gather emotional heat and take on lots of energy. If you're still facing the situation, or something else bothersome happens with the same person—bang! At some point, it's likely that you will explode either on the issue or some other thing that may crop up.

2. That jerk had it coming! Some people are convinced that the world is packed with jerks. Many people were taught "don't get mad, get even!" This give-him-a-taste-of-his-own-medicine is not an excuse for your bad behavior—ever. It can also bring out aggression in the other person.

I heard this story: "I caught my future mother-in-law listening in to a very personal conversation I was having with her daughter. I screamed that she was a bitch and stormed out of the house. I thought she deserved it at the time. But we're married now, and my relationship with my mother-in-law has never really been the same since that night. I said I was sorry, but I think she still holds it against me. She doesn't talk to me as much. She doesn't go out of her way to get me into conversations."

It's not surprising that his mother-in-law would avoid him. People will often hold it against you if you scream at them. Though it doesn't always happen, if you blow a fuse, you can incur permanent damage to a relationship. Even though the mother-in-law exhibited bad behavior, as an issue it was less serious than the screaming.

3. You thought you were being assertive. You may think you were assertive, but if you used angry gestures, self-discounting, or harsh language, you thought wrong. You may not have meant to be aggressive or passive, but you were. Why? Because it is very easy to become aggressive without meaning to. Later on, I'll give you lots of details and dos and don'ts for your verbal and nonverbal signals. The story that follows underscores why these signals are so important. I was behind a woman in the express line at the grocery store. A man in front of her had a full cart. The woman said, "Hey, you! What are you trying to pull? Get in another line!"

The man she yelled at was clearly embarrassed. He said he didn't know he was in the wrong line. This woman probably thought that because she spoke up, she was being assertive, But because she yelled, she had become a bully.

These days in the age of social media and electronic communication you don't have the benefit of nonverbal signals, and your words take on even greater importance. You may not intend to be harsh, but others may view it differently. A friend went to a concert and was very excited to have great seats. She was taking a lot of pictures and posting them to Facebook during the show, until one of her friends commented, "Enough already! We get it. You're in the front row." My friend's feelings were hurt. After an email exchange, the harsh commentator apologized profusely and said she thought she was being funny and said that she thought her friend would know it was a joke. But how was she supposed to know? All she had to interpret her friend's comments were her words.

The Price These Bungling Confronters Pay

You may mean well. You may think you're being assertive. You may think the other person had it coming, but that's no excuse for becoming aggressive. These kinds of people can also have low self-esteem and feel out of control. They often achieve the opposite of what they seek by inviting more conflict into their lives instead of resolving it. Again, not a pleasant or positive way to deal with others.

Four Negative Confronters in Action

Negative confronters have some common behavioral profiles too. Here are four to watch out for:

The Bully

Unfortunately, the kid who crushed your lunch box has grown up, is still a bully, and now works next to you or lives next door. This is the person who says, "She had it coming!" This person must get his or her way and will often become aggressive if challenged. He is frustrated and doesn't know how to express it other than through aggressive behavior. She wants to win. End of discussion.

Some of the actions in the following examples are hard to believe, but bullies will amaze you. Like the professor who gets upset when there are typos in his documents. He doesn't say, "Can you please fix this document?" to his secretary. He just jams the papers under her chin. You can bet she fixes them fast, but does she like her boss? I think it's safe to assume that she doesn't.

Also hard to believe is the boss who cursed at his employee and threw a coffee mug against the wall because he was not kept informed on an important project.

And the pharmaceutical sales rep who *had* to see the doctor. She refused to take no for an answer and walked into an examining room while a patient was present. As a result, she was instructed never to come back to that office again.

The Shouter

Shouters are a subset of the full-blown bully. This is the person who is not happy about what is going on and expresses displeasure by shouting and then shouting some more.

An administrative assistant told me this tale: "I was told to get new business cards for the telemarketing group. The regional director told me to change their titles to 'telemarketers' instead of 'inside sales representatives.' One of the senior telemarketers didn't like the new title. He started screaming at me about how I didn't know what I was doing and who did I think I was to change his title? He screams all the time."

Some shouters may approach a conflict with the best of intentions, but their behavior doesn't match their intentions. People get upset and lose control. And then they shout and shout some more. Later they feel bad about losing it.

The electronic version of this is the unhappy person who posts, emails, texts, or tweets in all caps. OKAY, WE GET IT. YOU'RE ANGRY!

They are also the people who rant online. Dave was on a local bike riders' news group but dropped off because there were two or three people who were constantly criticizing other bikers or people on their local bike trails. "I bike for relaxation," he said. "I don't need to hear about how a group of bleep bleep moms with baby carriages didn't get out of someone's way fast enough."

The Self-Discounter

This is the person who negates what she is saying through passive verbal or nonverbal communication: "Gee, sorry. Well, you know how sensitive I am . . . " or "This is probably just my problem but . . . " or "I think kinda, maybe, sort of, what's bothering me could be . . . " Or she says, "I'm offended by the comment," and the offending person can't hear her because she puts her head down and lowers her voice.

You got your guts up to confront but you negated your position, blamed yourself, or didn't get your point across. You're back in the land of the wimps.

The Displacer

This is the person who suffers in silence—for a while—and then bam! He ignores the real issue and reaches the boiling point and blows a lid about another issue. True feelings leak out one way or another, sometimes to areas of conflict that are safer. Alan, for example, says he cannot confront his wife about financial issues because he is afraid of their bitter arguments. Instead, he snaps at her for little things, like leaving dirty dishes in the sink. He gets irritated beyond what the offense calls for. As a result, she gets irritated at him for snapping at her. She's confused by his behavior. They end up fighting over issues in their relationship that aren't substantial or meaningful. Meanwhile, the real problem goes unaddressed.

Relationships suffer under the weight of displacement, sometimes seriously. It happened to two roommates who got along well until one of the women started having her boyfriend over all the time. The other roommate felt her privacy was being violated but didn't say anything. Then one day she discovered the woman had eaten her last frozen entrée without replacing it. They got into a terrible, door-slamming fight. Of course, the fight had very little to do, if anything, with the missing food.

Needless to say, one woman packed her bags and moved out. Both women were upset and hurt. They didn't talk for two years.

Sadly, my nickel jar overflows on this kind of story too.

So Who Are You?

The point of these profiles is to help you become more aware of some all too common negative behaviors. You may have recognized yourself in more than one profile. That's very common. Many of these behaviors overlap. For example, avoiders sometimes become displacers.

Hopefully you're getting a clearer picture of who you are as a confronter. Maybe you don't like it. Many participants in my seminars look glum at this point. If you're feeling glum, don't worry. There's help.

Now You Have a Choice

Regardless of your reasons for not confronting at all or for confronting negatively, remember that you probably didn't know there was another way to handle yourself. You didn't realize you were making mistakes. Maybe you knew you were handling yourself poorly, but you didn't know what else to do.

> *You didn't know about Polite and Powerful because no one ever taught you—until now.*

Once you acquire the tools for confronting positively—including WAC'em, the eleven simple steps to ensure positive confrontation, the dos and don'ts of your verbal and nonverbal signals—how you confront becomes a choice. You can choose to have positive confrontations. You

So Who Are You?

Reasons for not confronting or confronting negatively	NON-CONFRONTERS			NEGATIVE CONFRONTERS			
	Complainer	Avoider	Pretender	Bully	Shouter	Self-Discounter	Displacer
DON'T CONFRONT							
1. The other person must know that his or her behavior is inappropriate.	X	X					
2. I don't want to hurt the other person's feelings	X	X					
3. I can tell someone I don't like his or her behavior?	X	X					
4. I'm afraid of what might happen.	X	X	X				
5. I'm afraid of becoming aggressive.	X	X					X
CONFRONT NEGATIVELY							
1. I repress . . . and then blow up.				X			X
2. He had it coming.				X	X		
3. I thought I was assertive.					X	X	

can choose not to let any of the reasons or behaviors described here rule you. No more avoiding, shouting, blaming, being quiet, pounding your fist. No more feeling crummy for being a bully, a complainer, or a shouter.

And as you'll soon discover, not only do you have choices, but the choices you make have consequences. Sometimes huge consequences.

4

The Choices and Consequences of Confrontational Behavior

You now know the reasons why you may not be confronting or why you may not be doing it well. You now have a better understanding of who you are as a confronter. This awareness is a positive step. But you also need to understand the consequences of confronting or not confronting others.

Once you understand how your relationships, self-esteem, and professional image—whether you serve on the PTA or are a CEO (or both)—can suffer when you don't have positive confrontations, you will have a big incentive to learn and use Polite and Powerful behavior. You will want to try out these skills. Once you do, it will be hard for you to go back.

Before they learn about positive confrontation, most people simply don't think about the choices and consequences of confrontational behavior. They don't even understand that they even have or are making a choice. But Polite and Powerful behavior is a choice. There are other choices. I illustrate them below.

The Conflict

Here's a simple but common kind of conflict that has to do with sharing space—the loud talker. Loud talkers can occur in your office, on the commute home, or at a restaurant. When I use this example in my seminars, several people will comment, "I've had this problem too."

Suppose when your coworker, Alex, is on the phone, he talks too loudly in the next cube. It's distracting and you're having trouble getting your work done. You can choose to respond in one of three ways that we discussed in the last chapter.

You Choose to Be a Complainer, Avoider, or Pretender

Classic passive behavior. You don't know what to say and even if you did, you're afraid that if you said something Alex might get mad at you. So you complain about Alex, "That Alex is so annoying," to anyone who will listen. Or you avoid the situation or pretend it's not bothering you by going to the conference room to do your work, often missing important phone calls or emails.

I define passive this way: complainers, avoiders, and pretenders let their space be taken over by another person's behavior, which is like getting a table at your favorite restaurant and letting the waiter eat your dinner.

When someone is doing or saying something that you don't like and you choose not to say or do anything, you are being passive. This is what avoiders and pretenders do. Complainers will talk about the person's behavior to others but never to the person doing it.

Ultimately your passive behavior is saying that you value other people's feelings and rights more than your own.

Here are the consequences that you bring on yourself by not asking Alex to lower his voice:

Nothing changes. Alex's voice on the phone stays at the same volume. Why would he change? He doesn't know that he's bothering you because you haven't told him. Your ability to work is still impaired.

You feel bad about yourself. Of course you do, you're a wimp! You may want very badly to be able to confront him directly. You may promise yourself to "do it tomorrow," but this tomorrow's sun never comes up. You may try to pretend that the situation isn't bothering you, or that it's mature of you not to let things bother you. But this pretending only makes you feel worse. It will quietly and swiftly erode your self-esteem.

Your relationship with that person usually suffers. A woman once described how she felt about an annoying coworker: "Even hearing Karla's voice from across the office made the blood freeze in my veins." It's not that significant if you see Karla only once a year, but what do you do when Karla is a person you have to see every day? What if Karla is your boss, teammate, or neighbor? You can't wish her away. You are going to have to deal with Karla sooner or later.

The purgatory of passivity is resentment. It will form the way a puddle does, drop by drop. Then as the drops accumulate, the puddle of resentment becomes a stream. In order to relieve the stress of this growing resentment, you may start complaining or bad-mouthing Alex, telling everyone how rude or insensitive he is.

Relationships drown in resentment.

Or you may start to avoid Alex. This is a kind of purgatory too. Like the CEO who cut through a conference room in order to avoid an annoying underling, many people I have met admit to going out of buildings, around corners, up extra flights of stairs, walking or driving miles out of their way—all because taking the direct route could mean running into (and having to deal with) that person. However, there are no stairs in the world that will take you up and out of yourself.

Others may think of you in a negative way. Whiner. Wimp. These are just a few negative terms others may attach to you. You may be the most technically able person to lead your company's next big project, but if you've been labeled a wimp, the higher-ups assessing you may worry that you won't be able to get the job done or have the ability to handle conflicts that may arise.

Exceptions: When Acceptance May Be the Best Choice

There may be times when choosing not to do or say something may, at times, be the right and most positive choice you can make. You may choose not to confront for many valid reasons: it's not the right time or place; it's not the politically savvy thing to do; it's a person you will never see again. It could also be that the person may have a personality quirk. Consider these scenarios:

- Your friend is always late. It drives you crazy, but you've been friends for years. You come to accept this about her. It's one of her quirks. Why do you accept it? Because she accepts your quirks.

- Your coworker has been in a terrible mood all day. She snaps at you every time you ask her a question. But you know that her mother has been very ill, and the burden of care is falling on her shoulders. Even though the snappishness is bothersome, you realize her behavior is only temporary and out of character. You decide to say nothing.

- You're having a miserable, crummy, rotten day. And now your roommate is leaving dishes in the sink. But you realize that you'll probably feel better the next day. You decide not to confront her about the dishes while you're feeling so on edge.

- You work with a programmer who is legendary for both his brilliant code-writing skills and his temper. One day he blows up at you over an honest mistake you've made. He's shouting at you. He's pounding his fists. Though his behavior is upsetting, you decide he will only lose it completely if you try to confront him. You decide to speak with him at a later time.

But Keep in Mind . . .

As you learned in the last chapter, passive behavior isn't always qualified by an unwillingness to act. You may, in fact, be confronting someone but you may be doing it passively, like the self-discounter. You finally get up your courage to confront but hamper your effectiveness by making mistakes in your verbal or nonverbal communication.

You decide to say something to Alex, but you don't want to hurt his feelings. After he hangs up the phone, you stick your head over the cube wall and say, "I know I'm such a pain and you're going to think I'm a pest, but your loud voice on the phone is so distracting. I'm sorry, I'm having such a hard time concentrating . . . "

Why should you put yourself down because Alex talks too loud? You shouldn't, but people who do this are so afraid of hurting another person's feelings that they choose to demean themselves and their position instead. This is self-defeating behavior and it happens all the time.

Consider what happened to Rick, a clinical researcher for a drug company.

Rick was getting more and more upset with his boss because he was being given a lot of extra work without being compensated for it. So Rick decided to ask his boss for a raise. "I told him I had been working really long hours. He agreed. I told him I was handling responsibility beyond what I was initially hired for. He agreed. He told me I was a hard worker and he sure did appreciate me. Then he asked me how the project was going. I was in his office for a half an hour and when I came out I realized that we had talked about everything except my raise. I really never asked him for it. I guess I was waiting for him to bring it up, but he didn't."

You Choose to Be a Bully, a Shouter, or a Displacer

That Alex is jerk! How could he not know he's too loud? You get madder and madder thinking about how inconsiderate he is. You get so mad that you jump up, hang over the cube, and shout, "Can you please keep it down. You're driving me crazy!"

If I ask a shouter, "Why do you shout at other people?" the person may say, "I had to do something," "I can't help it," or "It's just how I am."

But when you confront someone and yell, scream, curse, put down, berate or insult, you are not simply reacting or following your nature. You are choosing to bring down an avalanche of negative consequences right on top of yourself:

The behavior may or may not stop. Alex may lower his voice. Then again, he may think that you're the jerk and he may raise his voice even more just to annoy you. If you intimidate or embarrass Alex into lowering his voice, remember that when people are attacked, they attack back. Alex may decide to get you back later in other ways.

You feel bad about yourself. This is the confusing one. You may have a momentary high after shouting at Alex and your self-esteem may surge. This feeling is what leads people to believe that aggressive behavior is okay. But trust me, it doesn't last. You have lost control of yourself and sooner or later you will realize this.

Your relationship suffers. Alex doesn't like to get yelled at. No one does! It is difficult to have a successful work or personal relationship with someone who shouts at you. In fact this kind of behavior often destroys relationships.

Others may have a negative impression of you. You may be considered a hothead, someone who "needs to be handled." Your coworkers or friends may view you as someone who has poor self-control. Alex may even be afraid of you. Again, you may be the most capable person up for the promotion but get passed over because of your confrontational style.

Exception: When Aggressive Behavior May Be the Right Choice

Of course, there are times when you may choose to be aggressive and this may be a positive choice, especially if you're under threat. Here is a situation in which a woman chose to act aggressively and had no regrets:

Grace, a photographer, was hired to shoot a church pageant. She had permission to be there and permission to photograph the event. The man sitting behind her either did not know that fact or chose to ignore it. When she turned around to take a picture, he grabbed her camera straps and started choking her with them. He told her she was not allowed to take pictures inside the church. He wouldn't let her go. Grace grabbed his tie, pulled hard, and said, "Get your hands off me—now!"

This man may not have meant to choke her, but he was choking her. He did drop his hands when she grabbed his tie. In this situation, Grace's aggression was appropriate.

Confusing an "Aggressive" with a "Positive" Confrontation

Both aggression and Polite and Powerful behavior respond to another person's bothersome behavior. This is what confuses people. Because they have done something, they believe they have acted appropriately.

Darlene described to me what she considered her own positive confrontational behavior. A woman on the same committee had pointed her finger and spoken rudely to her. Darlene grabbed the woman's finger, held it, and said, "Who do you think you are? Don't you dare ever point at me again!"

Darlene thought that because she had taken action, she had behaved in a positive manner. She didn't. She behaved rudely by grabbing the woman's finger and shouting back. She was aggressive.

This is a common misconception among people who don't know the Polite and Powerful alternative. They think they have only two options—to confront aggressively or to not confront at all. They believe that because they defended themselves or spoke up, it was a positive action. Taking action is only one part of positive confrontation. It's *how* that action is taken that is also important.

An Unfair Label

It's also important to keep in mind that when you have a positive confrontation, someone may unfairly label you as "aggressive." Maybe the other person doesn't know how to handle a Polite and Powerful person. Maybe someone is unused to, or unfamiliar with, this kind of behavior from you. (Maybe you used to be a confrontational weakling.)

You Choose to Be Polite and Powerful

Alex probably doesn't realize that his loud talking is bothering you. You get up, walk around to his desk, and ask him if you can talk with him for a moment. You calmly explain that when he's on the phone, he raises his voice and this is distracting you. You are not able to get your work done. You tell him you would appreciate it if he could lower his voice.

Polite and Powerful Behavior Described

I'd like to give you a simple description of what Polite and Powerful behavior looks like in action. Let's forget about the terms passive, assertive, and aggressive; as you can see, there's a lot of confusion about what people think these behaviors look like. You'll see why Polite and Powerful makes so much sense.

Polite and Powerful behavior in action means:

- You know what's bothering you.
- You know what it is you want from the other person.
- You understand your own position *and* the other person's point of view.
- You make a conscious choice to say something directly, respectfully, and powerfully.
- You use polite language when you speak.

The consequences of making this choice are:

The bothersome behavior often stops. Alex will probably lower his voice. Why not? Most people are not jerks who are out to get you. When treated with respect, most people will treat you the same way. There are no guarantees that you will get what you want, but Polite and Powerful behavior gives you the best chance for that or, equally important, for working out an alternative solution.

You feel good about yourself. Of course you do! You behaved in a way that was respectful to yourself and to the other person. You're not letting your negative feelings rule your life. You are in control.

Your relationship with that person can usually be maintained and can often get better. When you're able to work through your difficulties with others, your relationships at work and in your personal life are likely to improve because they will be more honest. When you confront Politely and Powerfully, you can stop secretly resenting the person. You don't have to ignore or avoid people. You can stop complaining and pretending too. Again, there are no guarantees, but Polite and Powerful behavior is your best chance for maintaining the relationship.

Others have a positive view of you. Here's a surprise—Alex may appreciate that you let him know what was bothering you. He may be impressed by your directness and willingness to speak up on your own behalf. (He certainly won't have a good opinion of you if he finds out you're bad-mouthing him around the office.) Polite and Powerful people are able to work well with all types of people and that's a quality promotable people share.

The Benefits of Polite and Powerful at a Glance

The chart below sums up the benefits and consequences of each of the confrontational choices you make:

Consequences of Confrontational Choices			
	PASSIVE	AGGRESSIVE	POLITE AND POWERFUL
Bothersome behavior	Continues	Stops/continues	Often stops
Self-esteem	Down	Up then down	Up
Relationship	Suffers	Suffers	Maintain/May improve
Your image	Suffers	Suffers	Can improve

It's hard to believe that anyone seeing this chart would choose to damage his professional and personal relationships, let his self-esteem run dry, or encourage others to think poorly of him. But every day, by not practicing Polite and Powerful behavior, that's exactly what millions of people do.

Many people who attend my seminars are stunned to make this discovery. I routinely hear statements like, "I just didn't realize this before," or "I didn't understand that I was letting my friendships suffer because I'm not able to tell people how I really feel."

When you have a certain way of operating in the world, including how you decide to confront or not confront, it becomes an unexamined habit. You aren't aware of how it affects you and those around you.

But once you see and understand your own behavior, you can change for the better. I have seen over and over again that a new awareness, even if it seems hard at first, can enable you to make a positive change in your life. Polite and Powerful behavior is the gateway to positive confrontation.

Once they realize how their relationships, self-esteem, and professional image have been suffering, people who want to be successful in business and in their personal lives are unlikely to return to their old passive or aggressive behaviors.

> **Be honest.** Think of the last time you had or wanted to have a confrontation. Which choice did you make? What were the consequences of that choice in your professional or personal life? Would you handle yourself differently now?

Polite and Powerful Is No Guarantee That You Will Get What You Want

Most people find they get what they want or at least some degree of satisfaction when they confront Politely and Powerfully. I wish I could guarantee you these results too, but I can't.

A confrontation involves at least two people. You don't control the other person; you can only control yourself. You don't know how the other person will react. You can make predictions, but it's only a guess. But this I can guarantee: no matter what the outcome, when you confront Politely and Powerfully you feel good about yourself and most likely know where you stand with that person.

Of course, you don't have to confront or even choose to be Polite and Powerful, but now it's an option you didn't have before.

5

The Jerk Test

You've decided that Polite and Powerful is for you. You're going to learn the skills of Polite and Powerful. You're going to speak up once and for all. No more jerks are going to get the best of you!

But before you do decide to speak up, I ask you to pause and take the jerk test first. This is important. Let's talk about jerks for a minute.

I think "jerk" is a great word.

It's strong yet not so strong that it's offensive. It's equal opportunity and gender neutral. Men are jerks. Women are jerks. Anyone can be a jerk. But how many people actually are jerks?

Probably not as many as you think. People behave the way they do for a multitude of reasons. Being a jerk is only one of them. Others may include cultural or gender influences, personal experiences, individual expectations and priorities, age, nonverbal communication, religious affiliation . . . I could keep going.

Often we are quick to make negative assumptions about the behavior of others. We don't understand what is driving the person who is driving us crazy. Ironically, in making snap judgments, we become jerks too. Once you understand what motivates the other person, you still may not like the person's behavior, and that's fine. However, it doesn't necessarily mean the other person is a jerk (and you're not either).

If you approach a confrontation thinking, "Wow! What a jerk!" you may be setting yourself up for a negative experience. If you've already decided that someone is a jerk, that means you feel he or she has treated you badly, unfairly, unjustly. You can easily end up behaving aggressively when you're upset. But if you approach a confrontation thinking, "Maybe this person is a jerk. Maybe not. I'll find out what I'm dealing with first," you are far more likely to have a positive experience.

Is it easy giving someone the benefit of the doubt? Not always. Our first impression often sticks, especially when we're upset. But it's worth it to find out if the person really is a jerk or not; you may save yourself from a negative confrontation. In fact, you may discover there is no confrontation to be had after all.

Take the Jerk Test

Here are seven questions you should stop and ask yourself before assuming that someone is a jerk.

1. Does the other person really understand the effect of his nonverbal communication?

People express themselves both verbally *and* nonverbally. They may have every intention of being Polite and Powerful but their body language may be conveying another message—and they don't know it.

Here's the tricky part. People will believe your nonverbals before they believe your verbals. The suspected jerk may not realize his or her nonverbal messages are confusing. People don't always match their nonverbal behavior with the intent of their words. Two creative directors were annoyed at their vice president, who would tell them "good job" but wouldn't look up from his iPad as he complimented them. "We're not always sure he means it," they said.

Then there are times when we have only nonverbal behavior to assess. A network engineer thought that a woman in his group did not take him seriously at meetings. "She always laughs at me or giggles," he said, "like my opinion doesn't count." He was quite upset with her.

After learning the skills of positive confrontation, he was able to confront her—without losing his temper. To his amazement, she felt amazed at his take on her behavior. She had no idea that she was laughing or giggling. She had no intention of discounting him. She thanked him for confronting her about it. Who else, she had to wonder, had she unknowingly offended?

Maybe this seems silly. Who doesn't know when they're laughing or giggling? But trust my experience on this one. I have taught and coached thousands of people about verbal and nonverbal signals. I can tell you, really and truly, people often don't know they're giggling, snapping gum, staring, crossing arms, over-smiling, chewing pencils, frowning . . . You name it, people do it, all the time. Like the woman who told me she didn't point her finger—while she was pointing her finger at me!

More often than not, these people don't mean to be jerks. They may have bad habits or they simply may not be aware that their nonverbals are sending a negative message. In fact, you may have this problem too. It is very easy to pick up distracting or annoying mannerisms. Yet, as we will see in Chapter 8, consistent verbal and nonverbal behavior is very important to positive confrontation, and inconsistency is often the cause of misunderstandings.

2. Was the interaction purely a digital one?

Many misunderstandings that involve email, texting, or social media sites occur because there are no nonverbal signals to help you interpret the person's intent or tone.

The director of a county library system discovered that his administrative assistant was infamous for terse and seemingly harsh emails, like, "The director needs to see you as soon as possible," which sometimes created the impression that the director himself was annoyed with various staffers. He was stunned to discover this (and he had to admit that he was not reading the emails first). When the assistant discovered that people found her emails harsh, she was mortified. She didn't mean to be a jerk; she was just getting straight to the point, not realizing that she needed to soften her words or explain why the director wanted to see someone, for example, "The director needs to see you as soon as possible to discuss some new budget numbers that he just received. What's a good time for you?"

When communicating digitally, you may encounter a technical glitch or you may get only part of the story. A Facebook post, "Wow! I can't believe you took your daughter to that concert," caused a misunderstanding between two friends. Alison, the mom who took her daughter to the concert, thought that Julie, her more conservative friend, was criticizing her for taking her daughter to see a pop star who had some racy lyrics. Alison felt that her judgment as a mother was being questioned, so naturally Alison thought Julie was a judgmental jerk.

In reality, when they ran into each other, Julie elaborated on her comment, explaining that she and her daughter had been at the same concert. Only the first sentence of her post made it onto Facebook. The second sentence was supposed to have been: "We were there too."

And then there's auto correct. Whole websites are now devoted to sharing the funny mistakes that can happen with texting. A friend was invited via text to his boss's home for dinner. He wrote that he was going to "barbeque some kids," but what he really meant was that he was barbequing some "ribs." While many instances of auto correct can be humorous, sometimes you can have a miscommunication that creates a misunderstanding. My hairdresser texted me that she was running late. I meant to text back "NP" for no problem, but it auto-corrected and read "NO." She thought I was upset with her.

3. What is the other person's culture?

In the United States, our village is global; our outlook is not. I know—I teach international etiquette. This is an area that leads to an incredible amount of misunderstanding. Whether you do business internationally or never leave your state, you *will* be interacting with individuals from different cultural backgrounds and communicating with individuals who are speaking English as a second language (ESL). I used to teach ESL and understand how difficult mastering English can be for many people. Words are important—with them we express our ideas and voice our thoughts. But an ESL speaker may have a limited vocabulary. He may not be able to get his thoughts across fully. We can also have a hard time understanding ESL speakers as their pronunciation may be awkward or their speech slow. Along with difficulties in understanding each other comes an opportunity for conflict, given a lack of cultural awareness on all sides.

Here's a simple definition of culture that explains why it engenders so much conflict: the beliefs, attitudes, ideas, and values that *one* group of people has in common. What is important in *one* culture may be of no consequence in another. What's offensive in *one* may be quite acceptable in another.

Most people, regardless of their culture, have a tendency to judge what is different as wrong. When I ask a group of Americans, "What side of the street do the British drive on?" most will answer, "The wrong side." If I ask a group of Brits, they will say the same thing.

It's not the wrong side; it's the other side.

An American sales representative had lunch ordered in for himself and his Indian customer. The meal included meat. The customer, like many Indians, was a vegetarian and was offended. Why didn't the sales rep bring in a vegetarian meal, he wondered? How could he not know I don't eat meat? The customer stopped seeing the representative, who had no idea what happened. Each assumed the other was a jerk.

4. Did the person really mean harm?

Most people do not set out to hurt others. But many people do become preoccupied and do not pay attention to what they may be saying, doing, or tweeting, and how their actions can have an impact on others. The Ann Landers column mentioned in Chapter 1 is a good illustration. The hair-flipping woman probably wasn't aware of her action. Hair twisting, mustache twirling, and nail biting are examples of things people often do unconsciously. They don't realize that what they're doing annoys others and can convey a negative message.

Think about it—why would anyone flip her hair into someone else's face *on purpose*? It doesn't make sense. You would have to be beyond a jerk to do that.

Years ago, as I was pulling onto a highway, a man in another car blew his horn and called me something a lot worse than a jerk. I had no idea

I had cut him off. I believed I had the right of way. He was so convinced that I was worse than a jerk. I was out to get him. I wasn't. I made a mistake.

5. Is it the person or the policy?

Many times we get upset with someone who may simply be following company procedures. We may not know it or like it but it's not the other person's fault.

A claims adjuster complained that people in his office sent him needless emails. "Why," he wanted to know, "are people wasting my time? I don't care who is in the office when. Why do I need to know everyone's vacation plans?" When he complained to his supervisor, he found out that some departments had policies that everyone was to be told when someone would be out of the office. Since his department followed this rule, his supervisor wanted to know, "Why didn't you know that?"

A woman wanted to work from home while her child was ill. She was upset when her boss told her she must use her sick time. When she asked her about it later, her boss told her that she was following company policy. It was a policy that she didn't agree with and that might be changed in the future, but until then, she had to stick to the guidelines.

6. Does the person use technology the same way you do?

Remember when the fax machine was the most complicated thing you had to deal with at work? (Or maybe you don't remember because you came into the workplace after faxes were already considered passé.) When it comes to technology, there is a learning curve in terms of etiquette and social norms, and where you are on this curve is not necessarily where everyone else you're dealing with is.

Sometimes misunderstandings can be generational. Digital natives, those born into our technologically complex world, often think that digital immigrants, those who have to adapt to new technology, can be, if not jerks, than really annoying and stubborn.

Marion, the volunteer director at a nonprofit organization, was an-noyed when Eric, one of the new college-age volunteers, was not answering her phone calls about a schedule change. Eric thought that because he was emailing her back, their communication was fine. As it turns out, Marion hardly used her email and didn't see his messages. I hear the same kind of story about texting too. Not everyone who has a cell phone uses it for texting.

Phubbing, which is the term for snubbing someone you're face-to-face with by looking at or using your phone, is a big source of conflict. When you leave your phone out next to your water glass at dinner or your note-pad during a meeting, you are saying to the other people, "If this vibrates or rings, I will drop you in heartbeat."

Yes, this is rude, but many phubbers don't know that. Before assuming someone is being a jerk, you may want to extend the benefit of the doubt. People do all sorts of strange and rude things when using a new gadget or new social media site, usually unintentionally. People can become almost addicted to their new gadgets and need to be reminded to unplug. Many people don't know that texting in a restaurant or at a school recital makes them look like a jerk. People don't realize that when they overshare dozens of pictures of themselves (selfies) on Instagram and Facebook, others find them annoying and think "jerk!"

Because social media and electronic communication can generate so much conflict, I explore them in more depth in Chapter 13.

7. Does the person have the same information or enough information?

We may assume that a person has as much information about a situation as we do when in reality he does not because maybe there was an oversight or a miscommunication. Some people literally "don't get the memo." Brett was on vacation when his supervisor sent around an email with a memo at-tached as a Word document clarifying that jeans were no longer acceptable in the office, effective immediately. When Brett came into the office on Monday morning wearing jeans, his supervisor thought that he was defy-ing the new policy. The reality was that due to a spotty Internet connection on vacation, he had been unable to open the attachment and forgot about it until he got to the office.

Four male friends always spend New Year's Day together: "Three of us have been in touch to make our plans. The fourth guy is not in touch with us during the year as much because he has an all-consuming job. We can't make plans without him. I have called him and he hasn't returned my calls. If we leave him out, he will be upset. But if we wait, we won't be able to get a reservation."

I asked him if he gave his friend the reason for the call. He said, "Well . . . no, I just asked him to call me back."

After realizing this, he decided to leave a different message for his friend: "Tom, we're trying to make New Year's plans but we can't do it without you. We don't want to leave you out so please call Jeff by Friday so we can make a deposit at the restaurant. Okay?"

Tom wasn't being a jerk, he just didn't realize the urgency. He called back by Friday.

To Let It Go or Not to Let It Go?

Once you realize that the person you think is a jerk may not be a jerk at all, you're in a better position to decide: either to let it go or to have a positive confrontation. You are more likely to be Polite and Powerful if you're not working on a negative assumption.

But What If the Person *Is* a Jerk?

Hopefully, you see that jerks are not as plentiful as you may have thought. Yet they do exist. If you do come in contact with a jerk, what can you do?

First, let me tell you what you shouldn't do:

- Do unto others as they do unto you. This is how road rage escalates into violence: "You cut me off, so I cut you off." This makes you a jerk back.

- Behave rudely. My friend's son Jordan was in a coffee shop talking loudly on his phone. As the couple at the next table was leaving, the man shouted at Jordan, "I hope you enjoyed your conversation; I know we did." Though Jordan was being loud, that was no excuse for the other customer to be rude. Jordan had no idea that he was being loud and would have lowered his voice had he been asked.

- Resort to old behaviors. If the jerk is really bothering you and you have to see this person regularly, don't complain about the jerk. Don't avoid the jerk or pretend the jerk doesn't bother you. Don't shout, bully, or displace either.

What You Can Do If You Meet a Jerk

- You can choose to ignore the jerk. If the person is a total stranger, why bother? Chances are you'll never see him again. (You'll see why this option becomes easier to choose further down the road.)
- You can choose to act Politely and Powerfully.

Taking Polite and Powerful action may be your best option, especially if the person is someone you see on a regular basis. Why let a jerk get on your nerves regularly? Why should a jerk stress you out? You can deal with jerks—as long as you do it Politely and Powerfully.

I hope that you now understand why Polite and Powerful is the positive way to approach confrontation. It's the choice with all the benefits: lower stress, better relationships, and improved self-esteem. At this point most people tell me they are firmly committed to learning all the skills that make up Polite and Powerful behavior.

So here we go. WAC'em is next.

PART II

Making
Positive Confrontation
Work for You

6

Don't Attack'em, WAC'em

n Part I, we focused on finding out who you are as a confronter. I explained why you will want to try Polite and Powerful behavior instead of what you were, or were not, doing before. Positive confrontation is a more effective and a less stressful way of dealing with life's day-to-day conflict.

So let's suppose that you've been having a problem with another person. You're not sure what to say or how to handle it. But you do know that you're tired of complaining, avoiding, pretending, or shouting. You're tired of not being able to tell people what you want from them. You've taken the jerk test.

It's time to confront the other person.

Except now you have an advantage. Now you understand that you have a better choice than your old behavior, and you're choosing it. That's great! But exactly how do you do it? How do you have a positive confrontation?

As I've noted, confrontation, even if positive, falls into the category of difficult communication/difficult conversation. For most of us, it's the hardest type of conversation there is. As you know by now, this is true because most people haven't been taught what to say and how to say what's bothering them in a way that's both Polite and Powerful. Once you know what you're going to say and how to say it, your most difficult obstacle to confrontation is removed.

WAC'em

Positive confrontation begins with WAC'em. Your first step to this better way of dealing with conflicts and difficult conversations is to learn this simple model. WAC'em contains an acronym. The first three letters stand for three key steps in gathering your words for a difficult conversation.

W = What. What's really bothering you? Define the problem.

A = Ask. What do you want to ask the other person to do or change? Define what would solve the problem for you.

C = Check in. You've asked the other person to change something about his or her behavior. What does the person think about it? You need to check in and find out.

Don't Attack'em, WAC'em

Don't attack people. WAC them instead. WAC them with your words. You'll get much better results.

You know that if you attack someone, you can make yourself look bad, you will make yourself feel bad, and the behavior that's bothering you will probably continue. But if you WAC the other person with carefully thought out words, words that are both Polite and Powerful, you have a much better chance of feeling good about yourself, projecting a positive image, and getting the other person to stop the bothersome behavior.

WAC'em is simple, yes, but it has been field-tested on men and women from all walks of life, income brackets, and educational levels—and it works! WAC'em will help you figure out what's *really* bothering you and what you *really* want from the other person.

Keep in mind that putting WAC'em into practice isn't as easy as it sounds. Most people have no idea how challenging it is to get their words together for a difficult conversation until they sit down and try. That's why it is really important to figure out what you want to say *before* you say something. This preparation helps ensure that when you do say something, what you say will come out Politely and Powerfully—not passively or aggressively. It's easy to choke on your words, get nervous, get upset, or even cry when you're in a situation you're not prepared for.

So prepare to WAC'em. Using each letter to guide and remind you, you will be able to choose your words deliberately. We'll look at each element separately and then put it all together at the end of the chapter.

The W: What's *Really* Bothering You?

Answering this question will help you clarify your thoughts. You need to be very specific when you decide on your W. Whether your confrontation is with your coworker in the next cube or your brother, what is it about the person's behavior or comments that you are having difficulty with?

Break it down: what exactly is the person doing or saying? Describe it. Here's some advice on defining your W:

1. Be specific. Don't generalize. Avoid words like "always" and "never." Instead, link the behavior with a specific situation. Yesterday Sean arrived twenty minutes late to my meeting. Natalie was supposed to pay the parking ticket by Tuesday. Dan comes home and puts his papers on top of the television and doesn't hang his clothes in the closet. Olivia didn't return my phone call or texts last weekend.

2. Don't label the person's behavior. He's selfish or she's inconsiderate are examples of labels. Think instead, "What is the specific behavior that's bothering me?"

3. Consider the effect the person's behavior has on you. This isn't license to say, "You're driving me crazy" or "You're being mean to me again." You need to define the effect without bashing or attacking the other person.

GETTING THE W RIGHT

Figuring out their W is not always easy for seminar participants. Here are two examples of people who thought figuring out their W was easy but were wrong.

Example I: Emily

"I am so sick of my coworker talking to her new boyfriend on the phone. It drives me crazy. One day she was on for two straight hours. My W is that she is acting like a love-sick idiot."

Where this W went wrong: In this case, the W—What's bothering me?—was personal rather than specific. Emily didn't stick to naming the

(continues)

GETTING THE W RIGHT (CONTINUED)

specific behavior. She made a judgment instead. If Emily goes into her confrontation packing this W, her coworker can turn around and say, "Who are you to tell me I'm love sick? You're just jealous."

The W should have been something like, "When you have extended personal conversations on the phone, it's distracting."

Example II: Henry

"When I give presentations to the sales department, the department manager always talks, laughs, and jokes. My W is that I want to tell him that his behavior is always rude, unprofessional, and a poor example to set in front of the workforce."

Where this W went wrong: Henry also got sidetracked by labeling the manager's behavior. Plus, he generalized, which is not going to set the tone for a positive confrontation. The W is found in the behavior: "Yesterday, during my budget presentation, I heard you telling jokes to Tom. This interrupts the flow of my talk and tells other people you're not interested in my opinion."

Always go back to the person's behavior. That's where you'll find the W.

The Trouble with Labels

Let's talk a bit more about this tendency we have to label others. If your brother is borrowing your car and returning it with an empty gas tank, this may seem like a no-brainer. The W—What's bothering you—is that your brother is selfish or inconsiderate. He may even qualify as a jerk in this situation. You think, no problem, that's my W: My brother is selfish.

Only, it is a problem. You've negatively labeled his behavior. You haven't described what he's done that has bothered you, and he may even have a different interpretation of his behavior.

If you confront him and say, "You're selfish," he can turn around and say, "No, I'm not. Just last month, I mowed your lawn," or find any number of reasons or excuses to explain away his behavior and prove you wrong. This is how good old-fashioned family arguments begin.

In this case, the W should specifically describe what your brother has done: he returned your car with an empty gas tank.

I Can't Fix "Unfair"

When seminar participants come up to me and complain about someone, I ask, "What exactly is bothering you?" They often have difficulty verbalizing their concerns. They tend to use huge generalizations to describe the other person's behavior. I hear adjectives like "difficult," "lousy," or "unfair." These are labels that tell me nothing. They can have lots of different meanings to different people and they're usually negative.

One person told me, "My boss is a lousy manager. He just gives me attitude when he seems unhappy with me." Another said, "My teammate is not pulling her weight." Yet another said, "My boss is unfair."

I respond that I can't help them fix "lousy" and "unfair" or any of the other generalizations. By figuring out the W, though, they have to be specific and clarify what they mean. So the comment about the "unfair" boss became, "My boss signed up my three coworkers for the training but he didn't register me."

That was clear! This person would have been able to confront his boss about that, if he chose to do so.

Notice—and this is very important—the W is not accusatory. You're describing the person's behavior without judging it. You have a right to comment on another person's behavior if it affects you. You don't have a right to verbally attack the other person.

Suppose you're upset with your sister-in-law because she hasn't hosted her share of holiday dinners. Listen to the difference:

Kara, you never host holiday dinners.
Versus
Kara, we've had holiday dinners at my house for the last three years.

If you were Kara, how would the first statement make you feel? Probably defensive, ambushed, or embarrassed. Maybe Kara honestly thought you liked having holiday dinners at your house. If you accuse her, Kara instantly becomes uncomfortable. This W does not set the stage for a positive confrontation.

The second W statement, on the other hand, does. You are describing a situation that's bothering you. You are not accusing; you are stating a fact as you see it. You are much more likely to get Kara engaged in a positive confrontation.

More examples of getting specific about your Ws:

> *You always make me drive.*
> Versus
> *For the past few weekends when we've gone out, I've done all the driving.*
>
> *I should have known you can't keep your mouth shut.*
> Versus
> *I heard from Jen that you told her Tom and I are seeing a marriage counselor.*

When you're working on your W, don't generalize. Don't bring up past grievances. Stick to the specific, immediate problem. Keep your W specific but simple.

Why Does This Behavior Bother You?

In addition to defining the specific behavior that's bothering you, you often need to clarify why it bothers you. What effect does that person's behavior have on you? This can be important information for the other person to have.

Back to Kara:

> *We've had holiday dinners at my house for the last three years.*
> *[Describes what's bothering you.]*
> *As a result, the majority of the preparation and clean-up has been my responsibility. [The effect it has on you.]*

Another example:

> *For the past few weekends when we've gone out, I've done all the driving. [Describes what's bothering you.]*
> *I'm not able to drink. [The effect it has on you.]*

Give It Up If It's Not Your Issue

When you start thinking about how the behavior affects you, you may discover it has no effect at all. If it doesn't affect you, then it's not really your issue. And if it's not your issue, why do want to confront the person?

Melissa once complained to me that her sister-in-law never cooked for her brother. I asked her if he was sick and unable to cook for himself. She said no. I said, "Well then, what effect does this have on you?" Melissa paused and then said, "None. I guess it's not my concern."

Bingo!

Alice complained that her boyfriend never did anything. Again, this is not a W anyone can work with. When I asked her, "What exactly is bothering you about your boyfriend's behavior?" she said, "He sits around and reads all the time."

Then I asked, "What effect does this have on you?"

"Well, I was packing for our trip and he was just reading."

"Do you pack for him?" I asked.

"No."

"Does he pack for himself?"

"Yes," she said, "but he waits until the last minute."

Again I asked, "What effect does this have on you?"

"None," she admitted. "I guess I just do it differently."

This couple may have lots of other issues, but this one, at least, has been resolved.

If You Still Can't Give It Up

There may be times when you choose to say something to a person just because you believe the behavior is unfair or unjust. This could involve a coworker who leaves early whenever the boss is out of the office. It drives you crazy because you think it's not fair. Or your neighbor parks in your condo's handicap parking spot. Why the heck can't she park somewhere else?

In these this kind of situations, you may want to say something because you believe an injustice is being done. I'll discuss this in further detail in Chapter 14.

If It Is Your Issue, Then Make Sure the *Why* Is Honest

As I noted earlier, honesty isn't always easy but it's usually better. If you make up an excuse about why you're upset, even if it is meant to spare the other person's feelings, you can create another problem. The other person can respond to the excuse.

If you tell Kara, "I feel like I can't do as good a job as I want preparing the holiday dinner," you open the door for Kara to say, "You do a wonderful job! Don't worry about it."

This isn't what you want to hear from Kara. You want her to respond to your real concern—that she is not hosting her share of the holiday dinners—not get sidetracked by an excuse.

This is why getting your W right—and being honest about it—is so important.

Expressing Emotion

Sometimes the effect of another person's behavior is how it made you feel. I encourage you to express those feelings when it's appropriate. Depending on your relationship with the person you may want to say:

I don't like it when you call me lazy. [Less emotion expressed.]
Or
When you call me lazy, it hurts my feelings. [More emotion expressed.]
You didn't call when you said you would. [Less emotion expressed.]
Or
When you don't call me when you say you're going to, I get scared. [More emotion expressed.]

Expressing Emotion in Professional Situations

If you have a personal relationship with the person you're WAC'ing, it may be appropriate to explain how his behavior made you feel. Often that's all he needs to change his behavior. But if it is a business situation that isn't highly personal or a person you're not especially close to, you may want to keep your W simple—here's what's bothering me—and leave your feelings out of it.

If you do decide to share your feelings, don't make excuses for them, just be honest about them. This is especially true in professional situations. I tell people, if something is really bothering you and it is a professional situation, you do have a right to tell the person how her behavior makes you feel—just keep it simple and offer no excuses. Do not give a lot of history: "When you criticize my work in front of other people, it embarrasses me. My father used to do this to me when I was a kid."

Just say, "When you criticize my work in front of other people, it embarrasses me." You are describing the effect her behavior is having on you.

Say What You Mean but Say It Politely and Powerfully

If you catch more flies with honey, then think of tact as honey. You are far more likely to get what you want out of a confrontation by being tactful. What you say can set the whole tone for your confrontation. Your choice of words really matters. Here are some important guidelines for choosing and using Polite but Powerful language:

1. Write down your W. What's bothering you? Put it on paper. This will help you clarify the issues. Achieving clarity is especially important in the beginning as you're getting your WAC'em feet wet. When you're upset, you may exaggerate or get defensive. Writing your thoughts slows you down, helps you focus on the person's bothersome behavior and avoid labeling. You can stop and change the words. You can edit yourself. Remember, this writing exercise is for your benefit only. You're not going to read it to the other person. In fact, you don't want to because we often write more formally than we speak. Later, I'll give you a sample WAC'em worksheet that you can use to clarify your WAC'em words. In Chapter 11, we'll also discuss when it's appropriate to WAC someone in writing—whether an email, a text, or even a good old-fashioned letter.

2. Avoid blaming, accusatory "you" statements. Compare the following statements:

> *You never tell me things.*
> Versus
> *I need the information.*

"I" statements are usually assertive statements. "You" statements are often aggressive statements. "You" statements encourage blame and generalizations. "I" statements encourage you to keep the emphasis on yourself. Remember, "you" statements can put people on the defensive. Notice the difference in how each of the following sounds:

> *You are always saying mean things. [Offensive]*
> Versus
> *I'm offended by the comment. [Polite and Powerful]*
>
> *You're getting too emotional. [Offensive]*
> Versus
> *I'd like to sit down and discuss this calmly. [Polite and Powerful]*

"You" statements are often accompanied by negative words. Negative words put people on the defensive:

> You *neglected* your chores.
> You *screwed* up my hair color.
> You *failed* to meet the deadline.

What do these statements do? They blame. Avoid negative words like: failed, forgot, neglected, wrong, didn't. They put people on the defensive. Try phrasing like this instead:

> I need your help putting the kids to bed.
> This color needs to be redone.
> Deadlines need to be met.

Positive phrasing will help you set a tone, an atmosphere in which the other person can listen to your point of view. People hear "you failed" or "you did it wrong," and immediately close up or get ready for battle. "I" statements combined with positive phrasing keeps the communication channel open.

3. Avoid harsh adjectives when describing the other person's behavior. Though you want to figure out what's bothering you, you don't want to use the word "bother," as in "You really bother me." Avoid harsh words, like "disgusting," "lazy," "selfish," "revolting," and "annoying." They also serve to put the other person on the defensive. If that happens, the chances of having a positive confrontation are reduced.

4. Avoid exaggerating or generalizing with "always," "never," and "seldom." These words are not conducive to open communication. The other person feels attacked. Instead of engaging in a dialogue, you put yourself in a position of having to defend the generalization you just made. This is not a positive way to start your WAC'em wording.

When "You" Statements Are Necessary

Sometimes a "you" statement can, when it's descriptive rather than accusatory, be what you want to say. Sometimes you will need to use "you" to describe the other person's behavior. There is often no other way to do it. Just make sure it doesn't turn into a negative statement.

> Yesterday you arrived at my meeting thirty minutes late.
> Last night you said, "I don't want to go."

Softening Statements

When you prepare your WAC'em wording, it's often useful to begin your W—what's bothering me—with a statement that will help put the other person at ease. These are called softening statements. They can ease the tension of a difficult conversation by showing the other person that you are extending the benefit of the doubt. These statements can make it easier for the other person to listen to your W. Some examples of effective softening statements include:

> I'm sure you don't mean any harm by this.
> I bet you don't realize this.
> I can see this was an oversight.
> John, I'm sure you meant no harm, but when you
>   call me "hon," I'm offended.

Getting Your W Right

As you can see, figuring out your W is sometimes tricky. But it gets easier over time. After some practice, you will be able to zoom in on your W just by asking yourself, What's bothering me? Don't rush in the beginning. Keep writing out your W's until the process becomes second nature. It's essential that you get your W right. Remember these points:

- Be specific. Describe the other person's behavior; don't judge it.
- Don't label or generalize—no "selfish," no "inconsiderate," no "always," and no "never."
- Understand the effect the person's behavior has on you.
- Use positive wording to express your W, including "I" statements.
- Don't use negative or harsh words, like bother, annoy, stupid, and so on.
- Use a softening statement to put the other person at ease, when appropriate.

The A: What Do You Want to Ask the Other Person to Do or Change?

Once you have your W figured out, it's time to move on to your A. What do you want to *ask* the other person to do? How can he correct the situation that's bothering you? This is our second letter of WAC'em.

You shouldn't just tell someone your W, what's bothering you, and then walk away: "When you let your dog run free, he does his business in my yard." You can't assume the other person will get what's bothering you. This is why you must clearly define your A before you go into a confrontation or have a difficult conversation. After delivering your W, you explain what you want the person to do about it: "I would like you to keep your dog out of my yard."

You should define your A beforehand. I've had people admit to me that in their excitement to confront positively, they forgot or neglected to prepare their A. If you confront someone without knowing the A, you will let the other person have control over the conversation. Worse still, there may be no resolution.

What You Want to Ask for Needs to Be Specific

Like your wording for the W, you must be specific about your A. If not, you may not get what you want. You may get what the person thinks you want or what the person wants to give.

Specifying what you want to ask the other person to do can be difficult. Sometimes it is harder than defining the W. We often complain about a person's behavior, but we don't always know what we want in its place. Clarifying what you want will help you know what to ask for. There isn't a wrong or a right way. Plus, deciding what you want or what's important to you is empowering.

Let's look at an example:

The manager who didn't sign up his employee for the training session that others were going to attend is a good one. The A in this case is "I'd like the training too." But remember to be as specific as possible. An even better A in this case is, "I would appreciate it if you could sign me up for the training in July."

If you don't say your A, which is, "I'd like to be signed up for the next training session," your manager may offer a different resolution: "Sorry, you can go to the marketing conference." But what if you want the training because it is important to your career development? Your A must be specific. The training class may be full and you won't be able to take it, but this represents your best chance of getting what you want.

When in Doubt, Wait

If you don't know what to ask for, don't confront yet. A marketing director for a publishing company hadn't yet thought through her A, and this is what happened: "I was talking to my VP and my employee came and stood at the door. It really distracted and bothered me."

She confronted her employee. Her W was: "When you stand at my door when I'm talking to someone, it distracts me." But she never told her employee what she wanted. Sometimes people can infer the meaning and figure it out. But sometimes they don't.

She never gave the A, which should have been something like: "I would prefer it if you would not stand there. Please leave me a note or message that you need to speak to me."

Because she didn't give her A, her employee stood in the hallway instead of the doorway.

Another example:

Your roommate plays loud music when he comes home from a night out. Your W: "I can't sleep when you play your music late at night. I have to get up early for work."

But what's late at night? You might think it's ten o'clock. But your roommate thinks it's midnight.

Your A should be more specific: "I would appreciate it if you wouldn't play your stereo after 10:00 PM."

Write Your A Down on Paper

You will get the same benefit from writing down your A as you do from writing down your W—it will help clarify your thoughts.

To get started, begin your sentences with "I would prefer . . . " or "I want . . . " or "I would like . . . " Even a simple "please" is a fine start. Like softening statements, these kinds of openings will help create an atmosphere in which the other person can listen to you.

Deciding How Direct You Should Be

Depending on your relationship with the person or the seriousness of the situation, you may choose to be very direct or less so.

When you're very direct, you're specific about the desired outcome: "I want" or "I have to have." This phrasing could be appropriate with a subordinate or an issue that is very important to you.

You can be a little less direct by expressing your preference: "I would like" or "I would prefer." This phrasing could also be appropriate with a subordinate or a person above you.

The least direct option is to soften your statements with a question. "Can you please lower your music?" or "Is it possible to? . . ." You may want to use this approach if you're WAC'ing someone you don't know or someone in a position of authority over you.

Remember, you need to decide how direct you want to be.

HIERARCHY OF DIRECTNESS

I want. I have to have. [Most direct]

I would like. I would prefer. [Less direct]

Could you? Is it possible? [Least direct]

Taking a Position Versus Stating a Want

The A forces you to become clear about what you want from the other person. A *want* states your desired outcome. A *position,* on the other hand, is much stronger and has more significance. A position has a consequence to it. Don't go from *wants* to *positions* carelessly or lightly. You're limiting the amount of give-and-take and the ability to work out a mutual solution. Don't state a position unless you're prepared to follow through.

For example, let's say you have repeatedly asked your roommate not to play loud music at night. Now you might say:

> *I would appreciate it if you wouldn't play your stereo after 10:00 PM. [Want]*

Versus

> *I would appreciate it if you wouldn't play your stereo after 10:00 PM. If you're not able to do this, I'll have to move out. [Position]*

> *Please visit Mom in the nursing home every week. [Want]*

Versus

> *I really want you to visit Mom in the nursing home every week. If you can't, I'll need to move her closer to us. [Position]*

Ask for What Is Possible

When you ask for what you want, it must be something the person is able to do or to give you. You can ask your coworker to get to your meeting on time, but if he's required to be at another meeting that ends just as yours is beginning, he can't possibly arrive on time.

Suppose you are standing at the airport ticket counter. Your flight has been canceled. You tell the agent, "I must be on the next plane." Well, if the next flight is already full, you can't get on it. You are setting yourself up for a bigger conflict.

Like defining your W, zeroing in on your A will get easier with time and practice. You will probably get to the point where you don't have to write it down. You will be able to ask yourself, "What do I want to ask the other person to do?" and figure it out on the spot.

The C: Check In with the Other Person

The last letter of WAC'em is the C. You will be happy to know this one is simple and easy. But we need this last step because you are only one part of the confrontation. Just as it takes at least two people to have a confrontation, it takes at least two to resolve a confrontation. You've stated both your W and your A in a clear, direct manner—*What's* bothering you and what you've *Asked* the person to do. Now you need to connect with the other person, and the C, which stands for *Check In*, allows that to happen.

The C is often a question that requires a response from the other person. It's important to know that the other person has heard you and you need to hear the other person's thoughts or opinions.

The C allows you to get the other person's reaction. The other person may have good ideas too.

Your C can be as simple as asking the other person, "Okay?" Some other phrases might include:

> Is that okay?
> What do you think?
> Can that happen?

When Your C Can Be Stronger

There may be times when another person's behavior is unacceptable to you. These are "no further discussions" confrontations and your C is stronger.

> Are we clear?
> Can I count on you for this?
> Do you understand?

For example, suppose you're in a client's office or out with him during a business dinner, and he starts touching your leg. This is clearly not acceptable to you. Your WAC could be: "It makes me uncomfortable when you touch my leg, and I want you to stop. Have I made myself perfectly clear?"

Joanne had to tell her aunt that she didn't want her teasing her teenage daughter about her weight. She was not going to compromise. She felt her daughter's emotional well-being was at stake, so she also established a boundary and stated her position: "I don't want you to criticize my daughter about her weight. If you continue to do so, I won't allow her to visit you. Do you understand?"

Putting It All Together

As I mentioned earlier, being interrupted is a common bother, both in the workplace and at home. Using this as our example, let's go through the W, A, and C using this as your conflict.

The W: What's Bothering You

> W: *It's hard for me to hear your point when I haven't had an opportunity to finish mine.*

Or

> W: *I've noticed that I am unable to finish what I'm saying before I'm interrupted. I don't feel listened to.*

The A: What Do You Want to Ask the Person to Do?

> A: *I respect what you have to say and if you ask me a question, I want you to let me finish what I am saying without interrupting.*

Or

> A: *I will give you a signal to let you know that I'm finished talking.*

The C: You Check In to See If What You've Asked for Can Happen

> C: *Okay?*

Or

> C: *Can you do that?*

Here are a few more examples of how to put your WAC'em words together:

Situation: Suppose you have asked your babysitter to put your children to bed by 9:00 PM and you find out later that she let them stay up until 11:00 PM.

> **W:** "I am aware that you let the kids stay up late last time. They were very cranky the next day."
> **A:** "I need for them to go to bed by 9:00 PM."
> **C:** "Will you do this?"

Situation: A manager was upset with one of her consultants for making negative comments in her meetings. She wrote down her WAC'em words and sent her script to me:

> **W:** "You may not realize that when you make negative comments in front of other people, it changes the dynamic of the discussion, like when you said you wouldn't complete the survey. When you said this, the others suddenly lost interest."
> **A:** "I would appreciate it if you would save those comments for me, individually."
> **C:** "Okay?"

She ended her email by saying that after she spoke to him, he agreed to talk to her privately.

WAC'em Words for Life's Most Common Conflicts

Remember the twelve common conflicts noted in Chapter 1? Here are WAC'em words for these conflict areas that my participants have created. These are real WAC'em words that people created for their real-life situations. These are *not* meant to be solutions for your situations. They illustrate how others have applied WAC'em to their situations. These examples aren't meant to save you the work, but I hope you'll be inspired by them when you create your own WAC'em words.

Revisiting the Twelve Most Annoying Behaviors Using WAC'em

1. Space Spongers

Situation: My coworker at the next desk spends vast amounts of time organizing his social life on the phone. It's very distracting (and his social life is more interesting than mine).

> **WAC'em wording:** "Since we sit so close together and there isn't much privacy, I can hear most of your conversations and they are very distracting. I would appreciate it if you could lower your voice when you are on the phone. Okay?"

2. Digitally Distracted Devils

Situation: Your cousin cannot have dinner with you without repeatedly checking her phone for text messages.

> **WAC'em wording:** "I love spending time with you, but when you read and answer your texts during dinner, it's hard for me to enjoy your company. Will you please put your phone away?"

3. Bad Borrowers

Situation: My roommate borrows my clothes and then leaves them in a pile on the bathroom floor.

> **WAC'em wording:** "I found the clothes I lent you on the bathroom floor. I am happy to lend you my clothes, as I enjoy borrowing yours, as long you can hang them up or put them directly into the hamper. Will you please do that from now on?"

4. Constant Complainers

Situation: I have a friend who often calls and texts me to complain about her life. I'm sick of having only negative conversations with her.

> **WAC'em wording:** "Julie, the last couple of months when we talk you've been very negative about things in your life. It's difficult to listen to and it brings me down. You have good things in your life

and I would appreciate talking about those things too. Will you try this, please?"

5. Interjecting Interrupters

Situation: I often meet my college friends for drinks after work. I love getting together and catching up, but I feel like I'm never allowed to finish a sentence without someone interrupting me. I can barely get a word out.

> **WAC'em wording:** "I know we're all excited to see each other, but I would really like to be able to finish my comments before I'm interrupted and someone else starts talking. Can we please try to do this?"

6. Callous Commentators

Situation: A coworker makes nasty comments about people and thinks that he's being funny. He hasn't picked up on hints that I don't like it.

> **WAC'em wording:** "I'm offended by your jokes. I don't think they are funny, and I would appreciate it if you would not say them around me. Okay?"

7. Work Welchers

Situation: A member of my team is not doing her share of the work.

> **WAC'em wording:** "You may not realize it, but I had to finish the part of the report that you said you would do. I know we're all busy, but in the future, you need to have your work done by the deadline we all agreed on or speak up sooner. Will you do that?"

8. Request Refusers

Situation: My neighbor's dogs run loose and do their business on my lawn. I even put up a sign: No Dogs Allowed. It really gets on my nerves!

> **WAC'em wording:** "I don't know if you are aware of this, but your dogs run into my yard and do their business there. I don't like cleaning up after them. Please take precautions so it doesn't happen again. Okay?"

9. Annoying Askers

Situation: A close and dear friend is heavily involved in an incentive business and wants me to join. I have absolutely no interest but she keeps asking. She doesn't get the hint.

> **WAC'em wording:** "We've discussed me joining your business, and I've said numerous times that I'm not interested. It's starting to interfere with our friendship. I would appreciate if we could stop talking about it. Is that all right with you?"

10. Social Media Menaces

Situation: A woman in my book group posts pictures of me on Facebook and other sites. I don't like it when people do this.

> **WAC'em wording:** "I know you may not see this as a big deal, but I am not comfortable with pictures of me being put on Facebook without my permission. Please take them down by the end of the day. Okay?"

11. Holiday Hasslers

Situation: My wife is always dragging me on vacations to sightsee in other cities. I want to go camping.

> **WAC'em wording:** "You have planned our last four vacations. I have enjoyed being with you on these trips, but I miss camping. This year, I would like to plan our vacation and have it include camping. What do you think?"

12. Gruesome Groomers

Situation: My coworker wears so much aftershave that my eyes water when I'm around him.

> **WAC'em wording:** "I seem to be allergic to your aftershave. My head gets stuffy and my nose runs after a few minutes with you. Please don't wear it the days we will be together. Can you do that?"

MORE WAC'EM WORDS FOR COMMON CONFLICTS THAT DRIVE YOU NUTS

Situation: My wife listens to my messages on our home voice mail, and does not save them, and forgets to tell me about them for several days, if at all.

WAC'em wording: "Sweetie, when I don't get my messages, I can't respond to people and it makes me look irresponsible and rude. I really need to get them. Will you please save them in the future?"

Situation: My husband did not call and he was late.

WAC'em wording: "When I wake up in the middle of the night and I don't know where you are, god-awful thoughts go through my head. Please call from now on if you are going to be late. Okay?"

Situation: My coworker routinely makes appointments with me, but he either is late or doesn't show up at all.

WAC'em wording: "When we have an appointment I set aside time for you. And when you don't come or are late, it messes up my schedule. In the future please be on time, or let me know if you are going to be late so I can reschedule."

Situation: A coworker that I had to work closely with was saying unkind things about me behind my back to other coworkers.

WAC'em wording: "It's been brought to my attention that negative comments were made about me to our teammates. If you have any personal or professional comments about me, I prefer that you come directly to me. Can you do that?"

Situation: My boyfriend texts and drives.

WAC'em wording: "I'm really scared when you text and drive. You almost hit a car yesterday. Please don't do it when you are with or without me. Promise me you'll do this."

(continues)

*MORE WAC'EM WORDS FOR COMMON CONFLICTS
THAT DRIVE YOU NUTS (CONTINUED)*

One of my favorite WAC'em examples comes from a woman who was reading the first edition of *The Power of Positive Confrontation* in the library and was being distracted by someone's music. She emailed me her WAC'em experience:

Instead of just sitting there being annoyed, I thought, Why don't I try the WAC'em approach with this guy? What do I have to lose? Well, I gathered my thoughts, walked up to him, and said, "Excuse me, you probably don't realize this but I can hear your music over at my table. Would you mind turning it down? Thanks." Remarkably, he did just that and didn't seem put off by my request at all.

Working with WAC'em

WAC'em is not a rigid model. You'll find as you WAC people instead of attacking them, it gets easier to quickly zero in on your W's and A's. There may be times when you just use individual parts of this because that is all that is necessary.

Just Using the W

Sometimes just stating that something is bothering you—without attacking the person—is all that is needed. Sometimes just being able to express your displeasure is sufficient to get your point across. And being able to express yourself is vitally important in building your self-esteem.

"I worry when I don't get a phone call from you." This may be all you need to say. You don't need to ask for anything. The other person understands what's bothering you and what it takes to fix the situation.

Just Using the A

Sometimes just stating what you want without attacking the person is all you need to do. "Please ask me before you borrow my power tools."

You don't need to go into the whole explanation. In this case, the W is obvious.

Just using the A can help with on-the-spot issues. Quickly ask yourself, "What do I want to ask for." Examples:

- If someone is not arriving on time to your meetings, the W is pretty clear. What do you want that person to do in the future? "I need you to be at the meeting by 10:05 at the latest."

- If you are not being told the priorities of your assignments, what do you want your manager to do? "When I get an assignment from you, I also need to be given its priority."

- Patricia is a high-level senior researcher in manufacturing. She held a meeting in the United States with her European counterparts. She had asked a patent attorney to address the group. While he was talking he referred to her as "honey." One of the Europeans laughed. She had to do something immediately. There was no time for WAC'em. She simply and calmly said her A: "Tom, I don't want to be called honey."

Not Using WAC'em

The examples I have used in this chapter may sound simple. But for those of us who encounter situations like these day after day, they're not. We tend to think that our own problems are truly exceptional. Sometimes they are. But I hear the same kinds of stories every week. In fact, we all have variations on the same conflicts that need to be addressed.

And sometimes the outcome of not taking a Polite and Powerful approach to a conflict can be extreme.

A woman told me that her coworker, Andrea, kept complaining that their manager assigned her more work than he gave the other employees in the department. Yet Andrea didn't confront him. She got so frustrated she quit and left the company. She left a good job and a good company because she didn't know how to confront her superior.

Andrea was probably afraid to say something. But since the consequence that most people fear, losing their job, occurred anyway, what would she have lost if she had WAC'ed her boss? Nothing. And she might have gained a lot. Many managers and supervisors are just waiting for you to say something.

Two WAC'em Practice Aids

During my seminars, I give people WAC'em worksheets to help them prepare for a Polite and Powerful confrontation. As I mentioned before, when you are new to positive confrontation, writing down your words can help you clarify what to say.

However, I developed the worksheet because many people needed additional help, first to clearly define the other person's bothersome or annoying behavior, and then figure out what they wanted to ask for.

There are two parts to the worksheet, which is reproduced on pages 96–97. You can use it as a guide to create one of your own:

1. Analyze the situation. This step is at the top of the sheet and it helps you figure out what is really bothering you. You are not thinking about what you are going to say yet. You are trying to figure out the situation. As I have said, this is not always easy as we are quick to make judgments, such as "my colleague is disrespecting me" or "my boss is a jerk." What does that mean? You will want to jot down just key words in this upper box—words that are specific and focus on behavior. As a result, you are less likely to become emotional.

2. Prepare your words. This step is at the bottom of the sheet. You are now creating the words that you want to say. Use the information from the top of the sheet to script your words in the space below. As I explained earlier in the chapter, writing your words can help you figure out what you want to say and encourage you to keep them calm, clear, and concise. Once you fill in the bottom part, you now have wording to practice. You don't want to read your script to the person. Yet, by practicing, you know what you want to say, and as a result, your words will come out more conversationally and naturally.

Page 97 shows how someone used the worksheet to prepare to WAC a colleague who was going directly to the boss when problems occurred. You can easily create a worksheet on your computer when you start to write your words. You don't have to format your practice sheet exactly like mine; the important thing is to go to your computer, or grab a pencil and paper, and start writing.

And for a WAC'em Reminder

My seminar participants also receive a WAC'em card that they can put in their desk or carry in their wallets or briefcases as a quick reminder of the elements of positive confrontation. While they are gaining experience in having positive confrontations, many carry it with them to help them figure out their WAC'em wording. One account executive told me that he carries the card in his front pocket, and just knowing it's there stops him from exploding.

> ## DON'T ATTACK'EM, WAC'EM
>
> **W** = **What's** bothering me?
> **A** = What do I want to **ask** the person to do or change?
> **C** = **Check in** with the other person.

And you don't need to attend my seminars to get one. Just make your own on an index card. A human resources director who read the first edition of the *Power of Confrontation* told me she wrote the WAC'em steps on a Post-it-note that she keeps in her drawer. She used this "cheat sheet" to help her quickly prepare for a Polite and Powerful confrontation with a coworker.

You probably won't need to carry a WAC'em card around forever. The more you practice WAC'em, the better you will get at analyzing situations and then gathering your words for a Polite and Powerful confrontation.

Welcome to WAC'em and the world of positive confrontation!

Don't Attack'em, WAC'em Worksheet

The **Don't Attack'em, WAC'em** model will help you prepare for a positive confrontation.

ANALYSIS OF THE SITUATION

W
WHAT
What's *really* bothering you?
Define the problem.

A
ASK
What do you want to ask the
other person to do or to change?

PREPARATION OF YOUR WORDS

W
WHAT
Here's how I'll express it to the
other person:

A
ASK
Here's how I'll express it to the
other person:

C
CHECK-IN
Here's how I'll express it to the
other person:

Don't Attack'em, WAC'em Worksheet

The **Don't Attack'em, WAC'em** model will help you prepare for a positive confrontation.

ANALYSIS OF THE SITUATION

W
WHAT
What's really bothering you?
Define the problem.

—*Goes to the boss about our problems*

—*Frustrating*

A
ASK
What do you want to ask the other person to do or to change?

—*Come to me first!*

XXX

PREPARATION OF YOUR WORDS

W
WHAT
Here's how I'll express it to the other person:

—*You may not realize that when you go to the boss to discuss our problems, more work is created for both of us. It's frustrating.*

A
ASK
Here's how I'll express it to the other person:

—*Please come to me first, so we can work out our differences.*

C
CHECK-IN
Here's how I'll express it to the other person:

—*Okay?*

7

Eliminate Your Verbal Vices

WAC'em helps you get your words together so you can have a difficult conversation with confidence and success. I discussed verbal skills in Chapter 6 and suggested putting a positive spin on your WAC'em words by avoiding "you" statements and harsh words, and by using softening statements.

Because your verbal skills are so critical to a positive confrontation, we can't stop yet. Your use and delivery of language is a large part of the Polite and Powerful verbal package. What you say is just as important as how you say it. You don't want any verbal vices or bad habits interfering with your credibility and clarity when you're having a tough conversation with someone.

Self-Discounting Language

The use of self-discounting language is a big concern for those new to the world of Polite and Powerful confrontation. Self-discounting words or phrases can diminish your positive words and undermine your intent to be powerful. If you discount your words, it's easy for the other person to do so too.

I keep a secret tally of the number of self-discounting words and phrases my participants use during my seminars when they ask their questions or make their comments. The last time I did this, I stopped at twenty, and that was before the first break!

If you use self-discounting language, this is a habit you need to break. Otherwise, you will never be able to truly harness the power of positive confrontation. Here are the problem areas of self-discounting language to watch out for:

Wishy-Washy Words

These are examples of self-discounting words and phrases: I think, I hope, maybe, kinda, sorta, perhaps. In my seminars I use the following illustration: "I hope that perhaps this might be valuable information for you."

What? Do I or do I not believe this is valuable information? Yes I do! A better way to say this without self-discounting language is, "I know you'll find this information valuable."

One participant (who was a smart, high-level manager) said, "I don't know if I'm wording this right, and it's just my opinion . . . " (I didn't know either.)

I have heard sales representatives say to potential customers, "So, I guess I'll get moving on this." (Will you or won't you?)

"I'm hoping that if you look at the total package . . . " (I'm hoping too.)

Now compare the statements when the self-discounting language is used and then corrected on page 101.

Self-Discounting Language

A salesperson trying to sell me a new smartphone said this: "It's kind of convenient to have your camera like this; it might take better pictures that way." My thought was, "Is it convenient or not, and does it take better pictures or not?" Either way, I didn't want to do take advice from someone that indecisive.

"I Think" Versus "I Know"

The excessive use of "I think" is another tentative and self-discounting way of speaking. If you really know something, don't say, "I think . . . " Once

Self-Discounting Language	
SELF-DISCOUNTING	**POLITE AND POWERFUL**
"So, I guess I'll get moving on this."	"I'm going to get started on this today."
"I'm hoping that if you look at the total package . . ."	"Look at the total package. You'll see how it can reduce your costs."
"Perhaps we can find a solution to your problem."	"I'm confident we can find a solution to your concern."
"I'm thinking we should start here."	"Let's start here."
"I was hoping that perhaps you could email the data again."	"Please resend the data."
"We were kind of in a way embarrassed."	"We were embarrassed."
"Maybe we should go to another place."	"I'd like to try another restaurant."

when my son asked to go to a friend's house to hang out, I said, "I think it's okay." He responded, "Mom, do you think so or do you know so?"

I said, "I know so."

Why didn't I just say so? I do now.

"I'm Sorry, I Can't Apologize"

Often people say "I'm sorry" when they have nothing to be sorry for. A pharmaceutical sales representative said to a doctor, "I'm sorry to bother you today. I see you are very busy."

She didn't even realize she had said this until the doctor asked her why she thought she was bothering him. He added, "Don't you have valuable information for me?"

And she wondered why she didn't get a lot of time with the doctors she called on.

Don't say "I'm sorry" unless you meet the following criteria:

1. You mean it.
2. It is your responsibility and you have something to be sorry for. If you spill something or trip someone, be sorry.

Self-Discounting WAC'em Openings

Don't open a WAC'em discussion by apologizing or using tentative language. I encourage people to be polite—but polite doesn't mean you should discount your W or your A. If you begin a WAC'em by saying "I hate to have to bring this up," the other person is probably thinking, "So why are you bringing it up?"

Here are more examples of weak WAC'em openings:

Weak WAC'em Openings	
WHAT YOU SAY . . .	**THE OTHER PERSON IS PROBABLY THINKING . . .**
"I know this has been a bad time for you."	"It sure is, so don't make it worse."
"Maybe you'll think I'm being too emotional."	"Uh-oh, she's getting emotional."
"I'm having a problem with you."	"Get in line."
"I don't want to hurt your feelings, BUT . . ."	"I don't want you to hurt them either."
"I may be wrong."	"You're right; you are wrong!"
"I'm not sure about this."	"Neither am I."
"This is probably a dumb idea."	"It probably is."

Weak Endings for Strong WAC'ems

You don't want to have a weak closing to your WAC'em either. I have seen this happen over and over again. People will come up with a crystal clear Polite and Powerful statement and then ruin it at the end by adding, "I don't know" or "Gosh, what do you think?" This tentativeness undermines your ability to be powerful.

"I Don't Know" (But You Do!)

Women are famous for using this self-defeating, self-discounting phrase. Debra offered a very eloquent opinion about an issue we were discussing. She clearly knew what she was talking about, but before she finished speaking, she paused and said, "Well, I don't know . . . " Yet she did know because what she had just said was valid and made perfect sense. And she didn't even know she had said this until I told her. She was shocked.

I spoke to a women's physician group about this self-discounting tendency. An experienced doctor admitted that she didn't use "I don't know," but she realized that she added something else to the end of her sentences. When giving instructions to interns, she would explain a complicated procedure and then end the discussion with, "Oh gee, but what do I know?"

Her interns were probably thinking, "Well, since you're in charge, hopefully a lot!" Despite her extensive knowledge and experience, when she said this, it was if she were telling them, "I don't trust my own opinion or knowledge."

Why do women in particular have this habit? There are probably many reasons, many of which have to do with gender roles. Nevertheless, let's not get distracted by the reasons at this point. What you need to do is recognize whether or not you have this habit, and then eliminate this self-discounting language if you discover you're using it.

Self-Discounting Tag Questions

A self-discounting habit many people have is to tack a tentative question onto the end of an otherwise Polite and Powerful statement: "This is fair to both of us, isn't it?" (I don't know; you tell me.)

People will often deny adding these tag questions to statements, but they do, usually without realizing it, and as a result, undermine their WAC.

But Isn't the C in WAC'em Often a Question?

The C in WAC'em is often a question, but it's not a tentative, self-discounting one. Here's the difference:

"Amanda, when you leave uneaten food in the refrigerator for long periods of time, it smells up the whole lunchroom. Please clean your food out every two or three days. Are you willing to do this?"

Amanda will have to give you a yes or no. You need to know if she's going to cooperate or not.

If you had said, "Amanda, when you leave uneaten food in the refrigerator for long periods of time, it smells up the whole lunchroom. Please clean your food out every two or three days. What do you think? I don't know."

You're telling Amanda that you're unsure of your own ideas, and you're probably setting yourself up to not get what you want. If you don't have clarity about what you want Amanda to do, how can she?

Your indecisiveness may also frustrate the other person:

"We will go there, won't we?"

"No."

"But I have to go there!"

"Then why ask me if we're going if you've already made up your mind?"

"Well . . . you know . . . I don't know! Let's just go."

Other Verbal Problems

Self-discounting language isn't the only problem that hinders people during confrontations. There are a host of others to watch out for too.

Curse Words

I was brought into a company to coach the senior director, who cursed during his weekly meeting. The administrative assistants in the office knew not to answer their telephones during this forty-five-minute meeting because his loud curse words could be overheard.

Cursing, or swearing, at someone is not appropriate in the workplace, or anywhere else for that matter. Yet people do it. They get frustrated. They don't know how to express themselves so they reach for the first word that's convenient, easy to use, and easily understood by all. That's when some offensive word or phrase is said. These people look bad. If you curse, you do too. I'm not a perfect person, believe me. I just know how bad cursing is for your professional and personal image. People have not been promoted, and they have been fired, for cursing at work. As far as your personal life goes, I don't know anyone who enjoys being cursed out. Do you?

Filler Words

Filling belongs on the inside of a cream puff, not in a Polite and Powerful person's WAC'em wording. Excessive use of filler words is . . . um, um . . . totally noticeable. Have you ever listened to a presentation or a speech given by a person who repeatedly uses fillers like "um, like, okay, all right"? Filler words make listening to speeches and presentations painful for the audience. You're dying for someone to pull the speaker off the podium.

The use of an infrequent "okay" or "all right" is usually not noticed. But any word or phrase used repeatedly to fill a pause is distracting to the listener. People start paying more attention to the filler words than the content of what the speaker is saying.

You can find out if you are unknowingly doing this by using this simple trick: every time you leave a voice mail message, use the feature that will let you replay it. Listen to yourself. Are you overusing fillers? Re-record your message if necessary. This is a quick and easy way to evaluate your speaking habits; take advantage of it.

"You" Instead of "I" Statements

We considered the use of "I" versus "you" statements in the last chapter. I'm bringing this up again because beginning a confrontation with "you" statements is one of the biggest reasons why people are perceived as aggressive instead of Polite and Powerful. People simply don't realize how much better their comments will be taken if they use "I" statements instead of "you" statements. Occasionally you must use "you" to describe the other's person's behavior, as in, "You were two hours past your curfew." Otherwise, stick to "I."

Say the following aloud and listen to the difference:

"You" Versus "I" Statements	
"YOU"	**"I"**
"You're wrong."	"I disagree."
"You're not explaining it right."	"I'm not understanding."
"You're always late."	"I need you to be on time."
"You talked back to me."	"I need to have your respect in front of the team."
"You didn't tell me."	"I didn't know."
"You're in my seat."	"I also have 6C."
"You're insulting me."	"I feel insulted."

Wow, what a difference! Check yourself. Make sure you're using "I" not "you" statements. This is another good reason to write down your WAC'em words before you confront another person. "You" will be glad you did.

Sexist Language

Both men and women call females "girls." They're women. They should be referred to as such by both genders. People ask what's the big deal? If you're the "girl" it can be.

I've heard stories . . . like the woman who was temping in a publishing company. The publisher—the top person in this division—told her to "be a good girl and make a cup of coffee."

She was outraged! She Politely and Powerfully told him that making coffee was not a part of her job description.

Some people use the word "ladies." Ladies is better than "girls," but generally the preferred term is "women." A college newspaper typically referred to the men's soccer team and the girls' soccer team, until the women's soccer coach sent a letter to the editor pointing out the disparity in language.

Other potentially offensive terms of address include sweetie, bud, dear, sugar, dude, and big guy.

I once heard a funny story about a delivery driver who was WAC'ed by a woman in an office on his route. The driver would routinely greet the four women in the front office, "Hello, hot mamas." One of the women didn't like it and so she WAC'ed him: "When you call me hot mama, I'm offended. Please don't call me hot mama—regardless of whether I am or not." The next time the driver came into the office he said, "Hey, hot mamas" and then pointed to the woman who WAC'ed him and said, "Except for you."

Grammar Gremlins and Diction Don'ts

I've coached people and have had to tell them that their grammar makes them sound less intelligent than they are. It's true. It does.

If your grammar is bad or careless, try your best to clean it up. There are many great books, websites, and apps available for quick basic skill brush-ups. (I know a lot of people who use them.) There are also courses at community colleges and adult learning centers.

The reason I encourage you to brush up is evident in the next example.

You say to your supervisor, "I don't need no reminders we're on a tight deadline." Well, you may know you're on a deadline, but unfortunately you have just tarnished your message and your credibility by using a double negative. You should say, "I don't need to be reminded that we're on a tight schedule."

Lots of people make mistakes in how they use language and grammar. Lots of people know better, but as we now know, we all walk around with bad speaking habits that need to be broken. If you use "ain't," break this habit as fast as you can. Ain't taints!

I have a friend who used a good trick to successfully break a bad habit. She snapped a rubber band on her wrist for a few days as a reminder not to say "got none" instead of "don't have any."

Diction Vixens

Diction, as in the examples above, has to do with your word choices. And it's also your delivery and enunciation of those words. Delivery counts. We make assumptions about people based on how clearly they do, or do not, speak. One accountant, who looked very professional and capable, complained to me that he didn't feel listened to by others. After listening to him, I felt I knew why. He was a word blender and a phrase mutilator. He said, "gahead" instead of "go ahead," and "I dunno" instead of "I don't know." Plus, he slurred his words, which made it even harder, not only to listen to him, but also to understand him.

I shared my own story about being a former wimp and word blender. When I was starting my career, I was sent for speech coaching. After just meeting the coach, she said, "Start talking," and I started giving her one of my speeches.

She stopped me after a couple of minutes and said, "You're from the East Coast, aren't you, Barbara?"

I was afraid to ask how she knew. She said, "You look great, but you say 'gotta' and 'gonna.' You need to stop that. You jumble your words together and you sound terrible."

Though she wounded my pride at the time, she was right. It sounds terrible during a speech or presentation to hear "gonna" and "gotta."

Try it right now. Say the following aloud and compare how each *sounds*:

> *I'm gonna tell you about Polite and Powerful behavior. You've gotta have these skills.*

Versus

> *I'm going to tell you about Polite and Powerful behavior. You need to have these skills.*

Many people tell me that they make negative assumptions about others who do not use proper wording or who blend, mumble, or slur. Maybe this isn't fair. I can't fix the unfairness of the situation; however, I hope I can inspire you to fix your diction. Again, listening to yourself on voice mail is a good way to identify any bad diction habits you have acquired. Then practice speaking clearly and slowly. You can also try reciting tongue twisters.

Watch Out For . . .

Bad Diction Habits	
SAY . . .	**INSTEAD OF . . .**
Did you eat?	Jeet?
Sandwich	Samich
Them/Those/There	Dem/Dose/Dare
Did you?	Didya
Don't know	Dunno
What do you	Whaddya
Have to	Hafta

Identifying Regional Quirks

Everybody else says it: "So whads da big deal?"

Every part of the country and every major city has its verbal idiosyncrasies, whether in word choice or pronunciation. In many parts of the country, it's "crick" instead of "creek" or "bawler" instead of "boiler." In the Philadelphia area, where I'm from, people say "youse can come over," instead of "you can come over."

This aspect of your diction may seem inconsequential, but as I've pointed out, these kinds of things can undermine the effectiveness of your WAC'em words and your image in general. Remember, the hometown folks might not notice, but what if you're called on to speak to people in other cities? Others will notice your differences and may find your vernacular confusing or distracting. Or they have a hard time understanding what you're saying.

Big Words Because They're Big

> *If you can't explain it simply, you don't understand it well enough.*
>
> —ALBERT EINSTEIN

I had a professor in college who used to challenge us every time we used what he considered an unnecessarily big or "ten cent" word. I thought he was a bit of a kook until I got out into the working world and encountered the big-word droppers. I'm not saying that you don't want to have a powerful vocabulary. However, using a word the other person isn't familiar with can cause confusion or make him feel that you're putting him down, or both. This isn't polite and it isn't powerful. You don't need to get your confidence from a dictionary; your Polite and Powerful skills and practice will give you the confidence you need for a positive confrontation.

Be yourself (with good grammar and diction) and keep it simple.

Simple Words Are Best	
INSTEAD OF . . .	**USE . . .**
Ameliorate	Improve
Solicit	Ask
Endeavor	Try
Peruse	Read or review
Terminate	End
Supersedes	Replaces
Purports	Claims
Assimilate	Learn
Utilize	Use
Reiterate	Repeat

Another piece of advice: if you're not sure how to pronounce a word, skip it.

And if you're not sure exactly what a word means, skip that one too. At a regional meeting, the CEO told the audience, "We're going to have the penultimate year in 2014!" (Penultimate is not a synonym for ultimate; it means "next to last." Oops!)

Use Polite Language—Always

If you think I'm a politeness pusher because I also teach business etiquette, you are right. One of the reasons I enjoy my job enough to write a book about it is that I have often seen how the little things, like saying "I appreciate your thinking of me," "no thank you, maybe another time," and even "good morning" can affect the way people respond to you.

Tune in to the words you routinely use and how you say them. Hear what you're saying to others. When you catch yourself making one of the mistakes discussed here, write it down. Keep a log. Awareness goes a long, long way in breaking bad verbal habits. Once you break a habit, move on to the next area. In a few weeks you'll be surprised at your progress.

8

Vital Nonverbals

You have just learned how important your verbals are for the success of your WAC'em wording. But what you don't say will often impact the outcome of your confrontation and difficult conversation too. In other words, your nonverbals are also at work affecting the way the other person is receiving your WAC'em wording.

Have you ever seen or heard someone who:

- Agrees to do something as she shakes her head no at the same time?
- Smiles while telling another person something negative?
- Gives a presentation while rocking back and forth on his heels repeatedly?
- Says he wants to meet someone and then stands with his arms crossed all night or never looks up from his phone?

These points illustrate what happens when your nonverbal communication doesn't match your verbal communication. When they don't match, you've got problems, especially during a confrontation. I illustrate this in my seminars by saying, "I am really pleased to be here," yet I am crossing my arms, looking down, and frowning at the same time. I don't look like I'm happy to be anywhere near this group—and they see it. Then I will pull out my cell phone and pretend to text. Again, they get the message: I am more interested in my screen than in them.

Many people have no clue how they're presenting themselves in terms of their nonverbal behavior. Nonverbal behaviors are habits. We do things that others might consider rude or gross without realizing it. We do things that make us appear timid or silly without realizing it. You may think you are behaving Politely and Powerfully when you are not. You may be delivering only the verbal part of your message correctly. Strong WAC'em wording is not enough for a successful confrontation. In order for you to have a positive confrontation, both your verbals *and* nonverbals must be Polite and Powerful.

Nonverbal communication encompasses your body language, your voice, and even your physical appearance. I will examine each area and explain how they can all have a positive or negative effect on your confrontations.

Who Are You as a Nonverbal Communicator?

Try to get an idea of where you may be in terms of understanding the signals or messages you're sending to others with your body language. In many of my seminars, participants perform a self-assessment on their nonverbal skills. It's amazing how high people rate themselves. I tell the group, "This is your self-assessment. Other people may see you differently! You need to know if a gap exists."

Of course everyone thinks I'm talking about everybody else.

There are people who resist me like crazy. It is really hard for some people to believe that they can seem rude, passive, disinterested, or even hostile because of their nonverbal behavior without knowing it. Like the man who pounded his fist and told me he was positive that he was assertive and in command of his nonverbal signals. And then there was the woman who was practicing her WAC'em phrasing and talked so loudly I had to back away.

To these folks, and to you, I say, "Don't tell me you don't do these things until you get feedback from other people that you don't do these things."

We All Make Mistakes

I am not immune to making mistakes, and I teach these skills practically every day. I believe I know what I'm doing with my body language when I'm up in front of a group. Yet when I was pregnant, I found out that I had been standing up in front of people and scratching my big tummy. I had no idea I was doing it until some of the participants told me. I appreciated that honest feedback.

Take the following self-assessment quiz and see how you rate yourself:

Nonverbal Behavior

	YES	NO	DON'T KNOW
1. I look people in the eye when speaking to them.	O	O	O
2. My facial expression is consistent with what I am saying.	O	O	O
3. I do not point my finger at others when I speak.	O	O	O
4. I speak loudly enough for others to hear me.	O	O	O
5. I do not giggle at the end of my sentences.	O	O	O
6. When talking with others, I do not play with my hair, tie, mustache, or jewelry. I don't crack my knuckles, fiddle with my phone, or play with change in my pockets.	O	O	O
7. I don't slouch, sway, or lean when standing.	O	O	O
8. I know the proper distance to stand when speaking with others.	O	O	O
9. I'm aware of what gestures I'm using.	O	O	O
10. I show others that I am giving my full attention by not reading, typing on my laptop, or texting.	O	O	O

If you answered yes to most of these questions, you *believe* you are aware of and in control of your nonverbal behavior. You may be, but I still encourage you to pay attention to your nonverbal behavior, just to be sure. You may even ask a trusted friend or coworker for honest feedback.

If you've answered no to most of these questions, you need to pay special attention to the advice in this chapter and make every effort to improve your nonverbal communication.

Again, the idea behind this self-assessment is not to make you feel good or bad about yourself. Just as you tuned in to your confrontational style, I simply want you to become aware of how you may be presenting yourself nonverbally to others.

You project an image; others perceive that image. You have no control over how others perceive you, but you can control what you project to other people. This is a hard concept for people to accept. I promise you that if your non-verbal skills are poor, they are probably holding you back in many aspects of your life, including your ability to have positive confrontations.

Think of it this way. Suppose your WAC'em is for a problem with your neighbor:

W = "You may be unaware that the water from your sump pump runoff freezes in front of my driveway and mailbox. It's dangerous. I have slipped a couple of times." (What's bothering you.)

A = "Please direct the water into a safer area." (What you want to ask the other person to do.)

C = "Okay?" (Check in to see if the other person can or will do what you've asked.)

This is Polite and Powerful language. But what if your head is down and you're looking at your shoes while you are saying the words? Or you're pounding your fist and raising your voice?

Your words may have been Polite and Powerful. But if the rest of you wasn't, then this disparity can affect both how you were perceived *and* the outcome of the conversation. As I've mentioned before, people will believe your nonverbal messages before they believe your words.

ON-YOUR-OWN ASSIGNMENT

Have yourself recorded annually, using your video camera, smartphone, web cam, or at a work training session. Role-play a work situation with a friend or pretend you're giving a presentation. Go back over the self-assessment quiz on page 115 to see how you're doing on your communication skills.

The Little Things Add Up

I tell people that the little things—your posture, your eye contact, your gestures, and so on—are little things until they're taken together. Then they help create a positive or negative impression of you, which will work either for you or against you. *You want it to work for you.* Cary Grant, the George Clooney of his generation, once said, "It takes five hundred small details to add up to one favorable impression."

You want to be perceived as a Polite and Powerful person.

Top Ten Annoying Things People Do with Their Bodies

1. Point their fingers at others
2. Lick their lips when speaking
3. Wring their hands
4. Sway
5. Have a very stern facial expression
6. Use too many gestures or no gestures, or stand with hands on hips
7. Pound their fists
8. Tap their feet or jiggle their legs while seated
9. Stare or make very little eye contact
10. Play with change in their pockets

BODY LANGUAGE BASICS

I had an eye-opening experience about my body language. I was sitting and talking with my mother in her living room. She brought up an uncomfortable subject. I pulled my knees into my chest, grabbed a pillow and held it in front of my chest, and then put on my sunglasses. I did all this without realizing it. My mother then asked, "Are you uncomfortable?" Only then did I notice that I had rolled myself into a ball and was trying to hide. We both laughed at how obvious the body language was.

—Catherine, seminar participant

It's critical to pay attention to your body language when you're in an uncomfortable situation. Are you telling people you're uncomfortable by how you stand?

William was at a cocktail party that he'd said he was looking forward to. Yet he was slouching and standing in a corner and not looking pleased. When no one approached him, he pulled out his phone and began to play with it. His body and his behavior were saying, "I don't want to be here."

Finally a friend went up to him and said, "Why are you acting like you're miserable being here? You're practically asking people to avoid you." And he was surprised by her comment!

Posture

The way you stand, especially while having a difficult conversation, reveals a lot about you. Is your stance conveying the image of a confident, Polite and Powerful person—or not?

Meet Mary Meek

A magazine advertisement for a new clinic featured two doctors. The male doctor was standing assertively—he stood tall, his feet were about five inches apart, and his arms were down at his sides. He seemed confident. The woman doctor was standing slightly behind his shoulder with her legs crossed, which gave her the appearance of having one leg. Her arms were also crossed. Both wore lab coats. The man had a collared shirt and tie visible; she had no clothing visible, giving the impression that she was wearing nothing underneath.

In my seminars I ask, "Which one is the doctor?" Time and time again the majority of participants choose the male. Many assume the woman is a nurse.

Both men and women can undermine their image with weak nonverbal behavior, yet I have noticed that women seem to do this more when it comes to posture. Women will often stand and lean their weight on one leg or cross their legs. Some even rest one leg on an ankle. Women also fidget with their hands or play with their hair. These behaviors convey nervousness. You are not going to be taken seriously while WAC'ing someone if you don't look and act like a serious person.

During my seminar breaks, I often ask a woman participant to look at her feet. She is often surprised to find that her legs are crossed at the ankles.

Men can stand passively too. They put their feet together, their hands in pockets, and sway back and forth. You can also hear them playing with the change or keys in their pockets.

Meet the Tough Guy or Gal

Some men tend to stand like a gunfighter in an old Western. Their feet are very far apart and their hands or fists are on their hips. In this stance, they are taking up a lot of space, which can be perceived as aggressive.

Though men are more likely to take aggressive stances, women too can take aggressive postures.

The "Polite and Powerful" Stance

Whether you're talking casually or confronting someone, you want to maintain a Polite and Powerful stance. Your feet should be parallel, approximately four to six inches apart. Distribute your weight evenly on both feet. Keep your shoulders back, but not way back as if you were in boot camp. Hold your chin up, but not way up. And unless you're gesturing, your hands are down at your side.

Gestures

Gestures bring your words to life. An appropriate gesture can liven up your conversation or help you reinforce an important point.

During a positive confrontation, it's especially important to be aware of your gestures. It's easy to let your hands or arms fly around when you're nervous or upset. If you're not in control of your gestures, you might seem nervous, or you might unintentionally convey a threat or appear to be aggressive. Your gestures need to be consistent with your words. You need to know what you are doing with them. And people so often don't. This is yet another reason why watching a video of yourself can be helpful.

Aggressive Gestures

The following gestures can send the wrong message:

1. Pointing your finger. Many people of both genders point a finger out of habit. And again, don't tell me you don't do this until you get feedback that you don't. I have had people tell me they don't point their fingers even while they are doing it in my face! Even a pen can become a tool of aggression if you're pointing it at someone.

I happen to know a sales rep with a nationally known corporation who lost his job because he pointed his finger at a VP during a meeting. He said, as he was thrusting his finger forward, "But I need that information now!"

The VP apparently did not agree.

A woman told me a story about how her young son demonstrated his counting skills. He showed one finger and said "one." He showed two fingers and said "two." And then with a moving pointing finger he said, "No, no, no."

Former president Bill Clinton used to point like crazy. He was obviously schooled not to. He now usually uses a pointed knuckle to punctuate his points. That's better because it's not perceived as aggressive. But if you want to point, point assertively, with an open palm and your fingers together.

2. Pounding your fist. When trying to make a point, some people, and in my experience men do this more than women, will pound the table. This is an aggressive gesture and can make even the most carefully prepared WAC'em words seem aggressive too.

3. Crossing your arms. Crossing your arms is not necessarily an aggressive gesture, yet it *can* be seen by others as offensive or closed. Sometimes people cross their arms because they are cold—literally. Other times, they simply don't know what to do with their arms.

Again, it always comes back to perception. If you're standing with your arms crossed because you're cold, the person you're WAC'ing probably won't know this. He or she may decide you're being defensive. What is the reality? Perception is reality. That person will respond to you as if you are being defensive.

Passive Gestures

If you're using nervous gestures, you will be perceived that way—and you are less likely to be taken seriously as a result. Nervous gestures distract from your powerful words.

1. Playing with your hands. People clasp their hands together and then rub them together. They crack or rub their knuckles. Who can listen to you when your gestures are so noisy?

Visualize making this statement to your manager as you're wringing your hands: "I'd like to take the lead on the next project." You are going to look like a nervous wreck. Will your manager really think you are capable?

2. Playing with things like paper clips, pens, and rubber bands. I coached a CEO of a very large and successful company on his presentation skills. After his presentation, I asked him why he was nervous. He said, "How did you know? I thought I was hiding it well." I said, "You twirled a rubber band the whole time." He didn't know he was doing it until I told him.

In one of my presentation skills seminars, a man was using a laser pointer. During the presentation, he proceeded to hit his leg with it. The class had a hard time listening to him. He didn't know he was doing it until we told him.

3. Covering your mouth. This is a common gesture where the hand is positioned to partly cover the mouth when talking. It's as if the person doesn't really want the words to come out. It is impossible to look powerful if you're doing this.

Eye Contact

Like gestures, eye contact is an important body language concern, especially in American culture. We don't trust people who don't look at us. Suzanne told me this story:

> I went to this doctor who was highly recommended to me. He seemed very knowledgeable and smart, except when I asked him a question. He looked away when answering me. He looked at the floor, the ceiling, his hands, his instruments. Everywhere except at me. I didn't care how good he was; I couldn't trust him and didn't want him as my doctor.

When people don't look us in the eye, we make assumptions about them that can invite conflict. We may think the person is not respecting us, isn't truthful or trustworthy. Yet people look away for any number of reasons—shyness, cultural differences—and don't even realize that they may be causing a problem.

You want to look people in the eye when you're speaking or listening to them. This is especially important during a difficult conversation. It's Polite and Powerful behavior. Don't stare the other person down either, as this is perceived as aggressive. You can occasionally look away, but not for too long. Failing to maintain regular eye contact can be perceived as passive behavior or create the impression that you are not listening.

In some cultures it is a sign of respect to look away (see Chapter 16 for more on cultural differences and conflict). But in American culture, eye contact is very important.

Seeing Eye to Eye

During a confrontation, you should be eye level with the person you're WAC'ing. If you're not literally seeing eye to eye, it can appear that the person who is lower, due to height or seating position, is like a child looking up to you as the authority figure. If you're trying to be Polite and Powerful, you need to be on the same level. I will often walk over to participants in my seminars when they are seated, stand next to them, and then look down on them. I ask, "Do you feel powerful?" No, they tell me; they feel small and powerless.

Psychological Advantages Are Neither Polite Nor Powerful

I know a man who is 6 feet 7. That's tall! He admitted that during difficult conversations, he used to purposefully move in close to others in order to intimidate or distract them. It worked for a while, but eventually he realized that it was causing problems in his personal and work relationships. He's now a Polite and Powerful man who sits down a lot to have difficult conversations.

Purposely towering over another person doesn't make you more powerful.

Making the other person comfortable and at ease is truly what a Polite and Powerful person does. People who are genuinely Polite and Powerful do not have to intimidate or artificially inflate themselves in order to gain a psychological advantage or to have a successful confrontation.

When it comes to being on the same level while speaking, many men are naturally taller than many women and therefore have a tendency to look down at them. You may protest and say, "It's not my fault that I'm taller." You're right, it's not your fault. Yet, if you want to be a Polite and Powerful and if you want to have a positive confrontation, it is your responsibility to be aware of your height differentiation. If you're initiating the conversation, and you're taller, it's your responsibility to correct it. You may want to sit down during a difficult conversation with a woman, or even a man who is shorter than you are.

124 • THE POWER OF POSITIVE CONFRONTATION

Facial Expressions

Your facial expression is an extremely important nonverbal signal. There are two big issues you need to be aware of when it comes to the look on your face.

1. Are you being consistent? Your facial expression must be consistent with your message. If not, people will believe your face before they believe your words. We have all seen newscasters who are smiling when they are telling us about disasters. It's not that they think the news is funny; it's that they are probably so conditioned to smile that they do it even at inappropriate moments. But it looks just awful, doesn't it? Women have a tendency to over-smile. We are taught from our earliest moments to please, be nice, don't offend. A man told me about the woman who smiled as she told him that he didn't get the requested transfer. She was sending him a confusing and mixed message.

Men usually need to smile a little bit more. I had a boss once who scowled while giving me an award. I left his office wondering, "Does he really think I deserve it?" Once I got to know him better, I discovered that this scowl was his default expression. He was a scowler by habit.

2. What is your standard facial expression? "You mean I have one?" Yes, you do. Your "standard facial expression" is my term for what people see on your face when you're listening to them or just not talking.

Jeannette said she didn't know she had a stern standard facial expression, yet friends and neighbors would come up to her all the time and say things like, "Is everything all right?" She would respond, "Yes. Why are you asking?" They'd say, "Because you look upset." She would say, "But I'm not!"

Jeanette didn't believe the feedback until she saw her wedding video: "It was the happiest day of my life and I looked miserable."

Now she believes the feedback.

I've had people sitting in the front row of my seminars and based on their facial expressions I am saying to myself, "These people hate me and they hate everything I'm saying." Yet they are the people who come up to me at break and tell me they love the seminar. They should tell their faces!

One man in the front of my seminar emailed me after the seminar to tell me that he "very much enjoyed" the seminar and did I have any feedback for him on his nonverbals? He had not gotten a promotion and was concerned. I had noticed him because he had volunteered to do a demonstration with me in the front of the class. I had been surprised that his hand had gone up at all. He had looked so stern during the class that I was surprised he wanted to participate.

Dressing for Confrontation Success

Your clothing needs to enhance your professional presence so people look at and listen to you. It can be a key area that determines whether you, and what you have to say, are taken seriously or not.

A PhD researcher came up to me after class and told me she was upset that she was not getting promoted. She asked me to help her with her WAC'em words so she could confront her director. Yet I wasn't surprised she hadn't gotten promoted. She was wearing a low-cut blouse and a very short, tight skirt. She looked like she belonged in a nightclub and not in a laboratory conducting serious cancer research. If I thought that about her clothing, imagine what her director was thinking!

I told her, "The first person who needs to be WAC'ed is you."

Later she emailed me and told me how much of a difference her new clothing choices made for her professionally. She was promoted and felt that people were taking her seriously for the first time.

I went into an aerospace corporation to meet with the human resource department heads right after their promotion meeting. They were discussing the engineer who again was turned down for a management position. I asked why. The engineer was not promoted because he dressed like a slob—old T-shirts, baggy and wrinkled pants—and senior management was afraid that he would not represent the company well since the new position required him to interact with international clients.

I also asked if anyone had said anything to him about the way he dressed. They said no. Because he doesn't know this, he keeps applying for higher-level positions and keeps getting turned down. I told them, "You need to be honest with this man and tell him what you expect from him if he wants to get promoted."

Even in today's more casual work environments, your clothing and grooming need to be appropriate to your professional environment.

Dressing for Conversations with Your Neighbors

What you're wearing might not matter as much when you're WAC'ing your neighbor. That said, I don't advise doing so in your bathrobe, pajamas, or bathing suit. Sam told me he was outside mowing his lawn when he saw his neighbor and decided to stop and WAC him about his hedges, which were growing uncontrollably and spilling into Sam's yard.

"I knew my words were right," Sam said, "but I sure regretted doing it that moment. I was sweating like crazy and had my shirt off. I just didn't feel confident."

The way you dress adds a lot to your overall confidence level. I tell people that before they WAC friends or neighbors, they need to feel comfortable with the clothes they're wearing.

Distracted Behavior

Always pay attention to people when you're interacting with them. Answering your phone, reading emails, and texting when you are with others sends a message that the person on the phone, or who you're emailing or texting, is more important than the people you are with. People think that they won't be noticed if they quickly read an email or send a text, but the body language, looking down and moving their arms, is noticeable.

A recent article in the *New York Times*, "Mayoral Candidates Wedded to Smartphones While Campaigning," mentioned that "mobile devices have introduced a new peril into candidate-voter interactions: distracted campaigning."

This article underscores just how distracting our mobile devices are if candidates on a stage in a high-profile election cannot resist the temptation to answer a text or email while appearing in front of likely voters.

Another *New York Times* article discussed a new trend in response to so much smartphone-induced distraction. When people are getting together for dinner, they are stacking their cell phones in the center of the table in order to pay attention to each other and not what's on their screens. The first person to touch his or her phone buys dinner.

The Power of Voice

A steady, calm, and audible voice is an important aspect of being a Polite and Powerful person. It's especially critical to have good control over your voice during a confrontation.

If you are going to get your point across, the other person must hear you. Sometimes, if you are not listened to, it may be because the other person is a legitimate jerk. But sometimes it is because your voice is easy to not listen to—too soft, too fast, or too loud.

A woman was trying to sell me her organizing skills over the phone. She wanted to come in and rearrange my office. Believe me, I would love to have my office reorganized, but her voice was so soft and weak that I didn't believe that she would be strong enough to be able to tell me what to do. I didn't hire her based on her voice.

Say It Loud and Clear

There are two key areas to remember about using your voice in difficult conversations:

1. Volume. Are you speaking loudly enough to be heard? Many people aren't, and this is true for both men and women, but especially women. The first thing I say in my women's seminars is, SPEAK UP. I teach presentation skills, and when people finally raise their voices, they feel like they are shouting. I have to assure them that they are not shouting. We can finally hear them!

A quiet young woman was attending one of my four-day seminars—positive confrontation plus women's issues. On the third day she shared a story. Before class that morning, she had stopped at her office, and her boss gave her an assignment to do on the spot. She had no trouble WAC'ing him: "I can't do that; I'm in a seminar." He responded by giving her additional work to do. So she said, "Don't you remember? I'm in the seminar and can't do the work." He then remembered something else she should pick up on the way back from the assignment.

She was starting to worry that she would miss the seminar. Then she remembered what she had been learning, and it dawned on her that perhaps her boss was *literally* not hearing her. So she stood up and in an unusually loud voice for her she said, "I'm going to the seminar now."

He said, "Okay, I forgot. I'll get someone else."

He had finally heard her!

2. Rate. If you're nervous about having a confrontation, you may increase the rate at which you speak without realizing it. Talking too quickly will make it hard for someone to follow your WAC'em words. Don't try to talk faster just to get more information across. If you don't have time to say what you want to say, arrange to pick up on the conversation at another time.

ON-YOUR-OWN ASSIGNMENT

You need to understand your vocal image. Though you can hear your voice on a video, you can be influenced by the visual. In the last chapter, I encouraged you to use a voice mail system to get feedback on the impact of your voice. Listen to the message you are leaving before you send the message, and redo it if necessary. You can also use the recording feature on your phone to evaluate your voice. If you do these exercises regularly, you will gain better control over your volume and rate. I give this as a homework assignment in my seminars and get the most positive feedback on it. People really learn from this exercise. Try it.

Stand Close Enough but Not Too Close

How close you stand to someone during a conversation is something you need to be very aware of during a confrontation too. In the United States, when two people are communicating the average distance between them is approximately three feet.

If you stand closer than the average three feet, you may be standing too close. People don't like space invaders. We can feel intimidated or uncomfortable when people stand too close. One woman told me, "I know I shouldn't get so close to people, but I like them. And if they back up, I just go forward." I had to WAC her on that one. She thought she was being friendly, but she was actually being rude. So pay attention. If people are backing up when you're speaking with them, you're standing too close.

Look but Don't Touch

Touch is a touchy subject in our culture. In today's world of sexual harassment awareness, people need to be cautious with touch. One woman told me that she simply touched a man's hand when he started crying, and he later told the rest of the office she was coming on to him.

And even if it's not a harassment issue, some people like to touch and be touched and others don't.

Though relationships vary, my advice is not to touch people when you WAC them.

What if your confrontation goes splendidly? It often happens that both parties are happy that the proverbial "air" has been cleared. Is it okay to hug or touch the person then? I've heard people tell me it has happened spontaneously out of relief.

In professional situations, you will have to use your judgment. It simply might not be appropriate to touch the other person. When in doubt, I advise you to shake hands. Men will often slap each other on the back. That seems fine to me, but again in some corporate cultures or to some people, it may not be.

Most health care representatives suggest asking "do you mind if I give you hug?" before any touching. That may work but consider what happened to Dave, a creative director for an advertising company:

"I had to reprimand an employee for not doing a job up to standard. I was dreading it because he had a reputation for getting dramatic. Whenever I had given him feedback in the past he became upset. I prepared my

WAC'em words to ensure that I was being Polite and Powerful but not harsh.

"Well, it worked. He took my comments very well. We both felt better. But as he stood to leave, he asked me, 'Can you hug me?' I didn't know what to say. I felt so put on the spot that I had to hug him, and I hated it! Now I have to WAC him about that."

Change Takes Time

Good control over your voice and visual appearance is an important component to successful confrontations. But you have to give it time. Try keeping a log of all the aspects of nonverbal behavior that we covered here. Tune in to your posture, your eye contact, gestures, voice projection, and so on. Once you are satisfied with one area, move on to the next. Habits can be hard to break, but stick with it. You'll be rewarded with good control over your nonverbal communication, and that will contribute greatly to your ability to have positive confrontations.

9

The Other Person

S o far, I've talked mostly about you. What's bothering *you*. How you can put *your* thoughts into WAC'em words. How *your* verbal and *your* nonverbal skills can affect *your* success during a confrontation.

Now we need to shift focus to the person on the receiving end of your WAC'em words. You've told the person **W**hat's bothering you. You've **A**sked the person what you would like him or her to do in the future. You've **C**hecked in. Each letter of your WAC'em is complete. Good job . . . but . . . just because you asked for something, doesn't mean the other person will give it.

Just because you have acted Politely and Powerfully doesn't mean the other person will respond in kind.

Just because you are not on the offensive doesn't mean the other person won't be.

Welcome to the other side of WAC'em—the mysterious, unpredictable, and exciting world of the other person.

No matter how confidently we think we know how someone will react to being WAC'ed—we can't really know. Even a loved one or a friend you have known since the beginning of time can surprise you during a confrontation. As noted in the last chapter, you can't WAC'em and run. It doesn't work that way. The other person gets to have his or her say too, whether we like what they're saying or not.

Though I don't know for sure how someone will, or will not, react, I can make some generalizations to guide you. There are six things that can happen:

1. The Person Agrees to What You Suggested or Asked For

We love when this happens! And guess what? It does happen. While there are no guarantees for successful outcomes, it happens more often than you might think. I hear it again and again—people are pleasantly surprised that what they thought was going to be a wrenching, horrible conversation wasn't actually that bad. Sometimes WAC'ing the other person will be so easy, you will be amazed. You may end up getting what you want simply because you asked for it. And once you've had a positive confrontation, you'll be encouraged to try it again.

Quick and easy conflict resolution often happens for the simple reason that the other person may not be aware of how his actions affected you. And when you approach the person Politely and Powerfully, you can get surprising results.

A woman who had taken my seminar told me how she agonized for weeks about telling the man in the apartment upstairs that his loud television bothered her. She practiced her WAC'em and finally got her courage up to talk to him. After she WAC'ed him, his reaction stunned her. He apologized. He didn't know that he was bothering her. He assured her that it wouldn't happen again, and it didn't. She was very pleased, yet sorry it took her so long to WAC him.

Another woman WAC'ed a coworker because he was telling her dirty jokes. She didn't like it and she wanted it to stop. He responded, "Sure, no problem. Why didn't you say something sooner?"

The other person, or people, may give you what you want because they recognize that it's the right thing to do. An administrative assistant said that this happened to her. She finally WAC'ed the others in her department about not cleaning up after themselves during their weekly meetings. It wasn't her job to clean up, but she had been doing it. Once she pointed it out to them, they started cleaning up after themselves.

When the other person, or people as in the previous example, give you what you want, make sure you thank them. Then, and I can't emphasize this enough, stop talking about it. Move on to other things.

2. WAC'em Leads to a Discussion

Maybe the other person disagrees or has a different opinion. The other person may have information that you didn't know about. He or she may have other suggestions or ideas—good ones—that you haven't thought about.

Sometimes when we can't get exactly what we want, the next best thing is to work out a mutually acceptable solution.

A friend of mine pointed out that being married requires constant give-and-take. I do a lot of negotiating with my son too. We often compromise with our partners and the people close to us to work out differences. (This is not the same thing as being taken advantage of or acting like a doormat.) But other people have wants that need to be respected too.

A group of friends met every two months or so for dinner. Paul didn't like Asian food, but the rest of the group would out-vote him and they'd end up going to a Thai or Chinese restaurant. Paul decided to WAC his friends. He told them that he wanted to participate and he wanted them to accommodate him, at least some of the time. They discussed it and agreed to try a new non-Asian restaurant every third time the group met.

It's vitally important to create an environment in which the other person, or again in this case, people, will express his or her thoughts so an honest discussion can occur. You need to take all viewpoints into account and work toward a mutually acceptable solution. If Paul had stormed away from his friends, he would have been aggressive. If he had stopped calling, he would have been passive. Instead, he Politely and Powerfully told them what was important to him. He gave his friends a chance to discuss it. He didn't demand that they never go to another Asian restaurant because that wouldn't have been fair either. What he got was his preference, at least some of the time, and that made him happy.

Here are some suggestions for handling a WAC'em discussion:

- Be patient. The person may have been caught off guard or may have difficulty wording his or her ideas.

- Listen. (See box.)

- Ask questions. Get more information whenever you can. Don't just ask question after question. Listen to the person's answer and respond if appropriate.

- Restate what you heard the other person say. You can use phrases like "Are you saying . . . " or "You're suggesting that . . . " or "If I understand you correctly, you're . . . " Restating is good for clarifying what was said and to avoid misunderstandings.

- Explain what you can or cannot do and why.

- Offer additional options, if you have them.

- Don't focus on any one thing to judge or ridicule the person about.

- Agree to a solution. This is a positive step, but don't make commitments you can't, or don't want to, keep.

- Agree to think it over and meet again.

- Agree to disagree. There may be times when agreeing to disagree is the best, or only, resolution. Suppose you WAC your sister because she takes your elderly mother out for ice cream, which she isn't supposed to have. You say, "It's bad for Mom." She says, "It's not going to hurt her once in a while." You both believe you are right. What do you do? As long as your mother's health isn't in immediate danger from eating the ice cream, there isn't much you can do except acknowledge that you have different viewpoints. You and your sister have your own ways of looking at the situation.

HOW TO LISTEN

Listen up! One of the things that appears consistently near the top on the list of what annoys people the most is other people not paying attention to them. Listening is a very important part of any discussion. Here are some suggestions for listening:

- You can't listen and talk at the same time. It's been attempted. There are people who swear it can be done. It can't. Stop talking. Let the other person talk.

- You also can't listen when you're interrupting.

- Give the person your undivided attention. Do not answer the phone, check your texts, work on your computer, or look away.

- Concentrate on what the other person is saying. Do not let your mind wander. Do not think about what you want to say while the other person is talking.

- Do not change the subject as soon as the other person has finished talking.

But I Really Want It My Way!

If only the real world worked so that you could have "your way" all the time, whatever you wanted. But it doesn't. Many times, you will need to discuss the issue with the other person.

3. The Other Person Gets Defensive

This is the person who gets WAC'ed and clearly doesn't like it. He or she may not want to deal with you or may deny the problem. Sometimes this person will try to make you feel bad for bringing up his or her behavior. This person will often make comments like:

> Geez, you sure are sensitive.
> Nobody else minds.
> I never thought you'd care about a little thing like that.

Don't get defensive in response. It will be tempting, but don't do it. You have to remind yourself that *you* are the Polite and Powerful person. This defensive individual may not have the skills or the same ability to treat and consider others respectfully that you now have. Don't apologize or justify your feelings. Your goal is to try to engage the person in a discussion.

Sometimes a simple statement like "I'm surprised by your response; I believe that this discussion can be helpful to both of us" is all that is needed to encourage the person to become responsive and open to a discussion.

Some people may be more resistant. Don't let the person change the focus of the discussion. Acknowledge his point and then bring him back to the main issue.

Katrina, an office manager, faced a resistant person when she WAC'ed her. One of the executives, a woman, persistently called Katrina nicknames, like Kit Kat, in front of others—even clients—and that embarrassed Katrina. Armed with her WAC'em tools, she approached the executive and said, "I'm sure you don't mean any harm, but you often call me nicknames. Please just call me Katrina. I'd appreciate it. Okay?"

Well, this woman was not happy to be told this. She said something like, "Oh don't be ridiculous. Nicknames are cute. Don't make such a big deal out of it. It's not that important."

But Katrina, knowing this woman's difficult personality, was prepared. She stood her ground and repeated a similar version of her A: "This is important to me and I would like you to call me Katrina."

This last part wasn't easy for Katrina, but she had taken a lot of time beforehand to boost herself up. One of the ways she mentally prepared was by writing down her WAC'em words and saying them aloud. She even brought her WAC'em worksheet to work so she could read it right before the conversation.

Though she was nervous, Katrina didn't make excuses or discount herself. She calmly repeated what she wanted. She was Polite and Powerful to the last word. Though this executive didn't verbally agree to stop when she was WAC'ed and quickly turned her attention elsewhere, she did not call Katrina nicknames again.

Here are three ways you can handle yourself in this kind of sticky situation:

Ask for clarification. Sometimes people say things and they don't really mean them as harshly as they come out. When you ask them to clarify, they have to explain their point more carefully and clearly.

After a friend made a really offensive comment, I asked, "Why did you say that?" He said, "I guess because I'm being a jerk," and that was the end of that.

Asking for clarification can also stop you from quickly and aggressively responding to the other person's comment. You are less likely to react emotionally when you have asked the person to explain his comments.

Clarification statements include:

Why are you saying that?
What is it about my request that's not working for you?
I understand that you think this is a dumb idea. Please explain
   specifically what is bothering you about it?
What exactly am I doing that is causing this response?
Help me to understand what you mean by "ridiculous."
What exactly about this suggestion is so silly?

Use a diffusing statement. If the situation is getting stickier, using a diffusing statement lets the person know you have heard him without necessarily agreeing with him. You don't want to argue about who is "right." You want to find a better way for both of you be able to continue the conversation.

Diffusing statements include:

That may be true. Still, I'm unable to meet the deadline by
  Friday.
Perhaps I did, though that was not my intent.
There may be some truth to that, yet we have to follow com-
  pany guidelines.
That's an interesting point.
That's probably true. My concern right now, though, is to clear
  this up.

But . . .

Notice that none of the above statements contain the word "but." This
little word can pack a big punch—it can instantly negate the positive statement that precedes it. For example, someone tells you, "You did a great
job, but . . . " Now you're waiting for the other shoe to drop and you're
bracing yourself for bad news: " . . . but you're fired/demoted/not getting
the promotion." People tend to go on the defensive when they hear "but."

Use "and" whenever possible. It's more neutral. "You did a nice job *and*
it would be even better if . . . "

Other words that can work include "yet," "however," and "although."

These diffusing statements are then followed with a statement rephras-
ing your point. Note the following examples:

A colleague says, "You promised that I would have the report by 3:00
PM." You have no recollection of saying that. Do you really want to argue
about it, as in "I said" versus "you said"? Don't get distracted by trying to
prove what can't be proven. Often you can resolve this kind of disagreement by using a diffusing statement: "That may be true *and* I can give you
the report by 3:30."

A friend of mine lost his glasses and went to get a new pair from an
optical retailer. The owner looked for his records but couldn't find them.
He told my friend, "You didn't get your glasses here." My friend said, "I
did get my glasses here." Each repeated his line about four times, before my
friend walked out in frustration and anger.

To stop the arguing, the owner could have used a diffusing line: "It's curious that I don't have your record. Let me see how we can get you new glasses anyway."

Two hours later the owner called my friend to tell him he had found the record, but by then it was too late. My friend had taken his business elsewhere.

Acknowledge the comment. This is when you acknowledge, or even agree, with what the person has said. Often a comment is meant to convey criticism, yet if you acknowledge it, there's no sting. It can even stop the conversation cold. This is a great technique to use during a difficult conversation.

Craig told me that his friend screamed at him one day, "You're just too sensitive about this." He looked at her and said, "Yes, I am sensitive about this." Her response was, "Oh, okay."

A sister loaned her brother money and wanted it repaid according to their agreement. He said, "You're so preoccupied about money. That's all you think about." She acknowledged the comment by saying, "Yes, I am concerned about money."

I saw a father jump out of his seat to scream at the umpire for a lousy call he made against his son. The umpire said, "You're right, I blew it." The father couldn't say anything else and practically crawled back into his seat.

Don't make excuses or try to justify your feelings, such as, "If you were in my shoes you would feel the same way." Just acknowledge the comment and move on.

4. The Other Person Gets Aggressive

This is often the bully's or shouter's response to being WAC'ed. But anyone can respond aggressively when you least expect it. What can you do?

- **Stay calm.** Take a deep breath. Tell yourself you can handle it.

- **Don't attack back.** Someone else's bad behavior is never an ex- cuse for your own. This can be a hard guideline to follow. If someone is yelling at you, don't you want to yell back? Many times you do, but as a Polite and Powerful person, you choose not to do that. As we saw in Chapter 4, you will gain nothing by this behavior. When you meet someone's aggression with your own aggression, you're giving that person the power to upset you. Aggression usually doesn't lead to resolution and can actually get you arrested or sued. I read about an argument that erupted between the dean of a business school and one of his professors. One of them shouted "shut up." The other hit him over the head with his briefcase! Their argument ended up in municipal court.

- **Remain polite and powerful.** Sometimes you want to let the person blow off steam or come to his or her senses. If you don't respond with aggression, you may well diffuse the other person. The person may just be having a bad day and will often realize she's overreacting if you stay calm. One woman told me she uses this Polite and Powerful statement with her customers and kids: "Screaming at me will not help me help you. It will only make us more unproductive." She says it works every time.

I went to a department store to pick up a suit that I had left to be altered. It wasn't ready. I was tired and hungry and I needed that suit the next morning. I kept saying (in a raised voice because I too lose it sometimes) "but you promised me . . . " The woman I was talking to obviously had read my book. She stayed Polite and Powerful. She told me, "I understand you're upset. I regret that it happened. Here's what I can do to help you . . . " She diffused me. She also offered to rush the job but couldn't guarantee the quality since she only had fifteen minutes before the store closed. I took her up on her offer and luckily the suit fit perfectly.

- **Use an exit line if necessary.** If the confrontation continues on an aggressive course, you need to shut the conversation down. You tell people, sometimes by your actions, what behavior you will not accept from them. Eleanor Roosevelt once said, "No one can make you feel inferior without your permission." You must establish your boundaries and you are the only person in charge of drawing your lines. Sometimes you establish a boundary by leaving. (If you're on the phone, you would hang up.) But if you do leave the room, don't storm out and slam the door. Use a Polite and Powerful line when you leave or hang up. I call this an exit line. Here are some examples:

"That's not the way to talk to me. When you can talk to me calmly, call me back. I am going to hang up now. Good-bye."

This is exactly what a sales manager said to one of her reps when he started shouting at her. He called back a half hour later and apologized. *Or*

"I cannot talk to you when you're screaming at me. I'd be happy to continue this discussion when you can talk to me calmly." (Pause to see if the person calms down.) If he is still upset tell him, "I'm going to leave now. Good-bye."

If you say you are going to leave, then leave. Don't linger by the door or in the hallway. Walk away. You will lose your credibility if you hang around and you may be tempted to reengage with the person.

- **Decide if the relationship is worth continuing.** If the person continues to deal with you in an aggressive manner, you need to ask yourself, "Is it worth it?" Do the benefits outweigh the drawbacks? I had a boss once—a virtual terror on two legs—who used to scream bloody murder at me. His temper was legendary. I stayed with the company for a while to gain some valuable skills and experience, but as soon as a good career opportunity appeared, I was out of there.

If you're having a problem like this, I'm not telling to quit your job tomorrow. You may want, or need, to stick it out for a while, but be aware of the negative consequences of maintaining the relationship.

WAC'ing People You Don't Know

A fear of aggression holds many people back from WAC'ing people they don't know personally. We live in an age full of gun violence, and so I can't just say, "Go WAC someone you don't know." I can't say this because I don't know what will happen either.

What I can tell you is that many people in my seminars tell me that it's easier to WAC strangers. This makes sense. They don't worry about hurting a stranger's feelings as much as they do a loved one's. The repercussions of WAC'ing strangers are fleeting because there's no ongoing relationship.

Is It a Safe or Unsafe Environment?

Before WAC'ing a stranger, however, you should consider the environment. Always use your judgment. If you're in a grocery store, bank, or crowded public place, chances are you don't have to worry too much about your safety.

Ed was in an excruciatingly long line in the bank when he noticed that a person was whisked out of the line by one of the bank employees. He didn't think anything of it, until it happened again. When it was his turn for service, he asked the teller why the other customers had been pulled from the line. Her response was that "they are regular customers."

Well, Ed was a regular customer too. Before learning WAC'em, he admitted that he might have "lost his cool." But he had learned Polite and Powerful behavior, so he used it. He asked to speak with the branch manager. He calmly asked the manager to explain the bank's policy on "special treatment for regular customers." The manager said there was no policy. When Ed calmly explained the situation the manager was apologetic. He said it wouldn't happen again.

In this situation, Ed was reasonably certain that the manager was not going to get aggressive. And he didn't. Ed was Polite and Powerful, and the manager responded to him with his own positive behavior.

Ed felt better. He had no guarantee that it wouldn't happen again, but at least he didn't feel "walked on." He had expressed his opinion and that alone made him feel better.

Again, in situations with strangers, use your judgment and your Polite and Powerful skills. In Part I, I mentioned a woman who behaved aggressively in a grocery story. Let's revisit that situation. If you're in the express line at the grocery store and the man's cart in front of yours is jammed with food, you can Politely and Powerfully let him know that he's in the wrong line: "Excuse me, you probably don't realize this, but this is the express lane." Maybe he didn't realize it. Then again, maybe he did. There are jerks out there. But at least if you say something, you'll have the satisfaction of having spoken up. And, assuming you don't lose your temper, you are going to look and feel better about yourself. Let the other person look like the jerk.

There are times when you should WAC a stranger as your professional reputation could be questioned if you don't, as this story illustrates:

A financial consultant took a group of prospective clients to hear a famous speaker. The event was a dinner held in a hotel ballroom sponsored by a financial association. Soon after they sat down and the speaker began his keynote, those sitting at the next table became quite loud and disruptive, which interfered with their ability to hear the speaker. As the host, it was the consultant's responsibility to make sure his guests were comfortable. He should have asked the people to quiet down, but he didn't take any action.

Maybe he was afraid that the situation would get out of control. But if he had been Polite and Powerful and the group didn't respond by quieting down, he could have gone to someone in charge of the gathering. Chances are, it would not have come to that. The rowdy group probably would have quieted down if someone had WAC'ed them. But the consultant did not try to control the situation and the prospective clients thought less of him.

If It Isn't Safe—Let It Go

If you encounter someone you don't know—on a dark street or in a sparsely populated area—or the person simply seems strange, having a confrontation may not be a good idea. The only thing I can tell you is to follow your gut. If you feel unsafe or something gives you the creeps, let the confrontation go and get out of there.

Marissa and Ben went to retrieve their car from a parking lot after a late dinner. When they went to the booth to pay, the attendant was on his phone and barely acknowledged them as he took their money. He didn't return their change. Ben called out that they were waiting for it. The attendant cursed and responded aggressively, saying among other things, "Can't you see I'm busy?" Both Ben and Marissa got the feeling that his fuse wasn't just short, but something wasn't right about him. Though they were annoyed, they chose not to say anything. They left without their change but were safe.

Road Rage

Road rage and aggressive driving are an unpleasant fact of life. People cut you off, refuse to let you merge, or nearly hit you because they're talking on the phone and not watching the road. However annoying and dangerous, these acts of rudeness do not give you license to gesture rudely or shout out of your window—dangerous behaviors. You can lose sight of the road or find yourself being targeted by the other driver. I know it's tempting to respond. I get as frustrated as you do when some jerk cuts me off. But then again, maybe the person isn't a jerk. Maybe he made a mistake.

And following a driver off the road to confront him about his driving is just plain asking for trouble. Let it go!

5. The Other Person Responds Passively

If someone gives you the silent treatment or "blows you off," you can't force the person to talk to you, but you can let her know what you think about her unwillingness to talk. Stress that it's important to you to work out your differences. You can say:

- I really need to hear your input if we're going to move forward on this.

- It's important that I hear your point of view. What are your thoughts on this suggestion?

- I assume from your silence that you agree with me and unless I hear from you otherwise I assume that you will be home before dark. (I said this to my thirteen-year-old stepdaughter. Boy, did she start talking fast!)

What if the other person doesn't say anything? What if he or she cries? Yikes! No one wants to be the cause of someone else's tears. What do you do then?

Maybe the person is truly upset. Maybe the tears are a defense mechanism or a manipulation to avoid talking. It's usually best to acknowledge the emotion and focus back on the topic. You can say:

> *It seems like this discussion is really upsetting you. That's not my intention. Why don't you go to the rest room and get yourself together, and then let's talk about it some more.*

Or

> *Why don't I leave for a few minutes so you can get yourself together? When I come back, we can talk about it further. Here are some tissues.*

6. The Person Says No (and Means It)

What if you are not going to get what you want—period? You have received a flat-out "no" from the other person. If this is someone you work for or who has greater authority than you do, you often can't force a discussion. "No" sometimes means "no further discussion."

Much earlier in this book, we considered one of the reasons why many people don't confront—they perceive it as too risky. They're afraid, for example, that they may ask for a raise and get a "no." Then what? Your manager or supervisor knows you feel underpaid and undervalued. Maybe the person is unhappy with you now. Before you curse yourself for speaking up, take a moment and think about it another way.

While there may be some risk involved in WAC'ing a higher-up, getting a "no" doesn't have to be a bad thing. You, like Jane, may end up with a different or a new alternative that you never imagined.

Jane was the office manager for a construction company. Upper management asked her to train the new controller for the parent company, which was the job she had been doing until someone new was hired.

At first she was a pretender. She told herself, "This doesn't bother me." But it did. She evolved into a complainer. She told her friends and coworkers about how unfair upper management was. "How could they ask me to train this guy? I'm doing the job now."

I suggested that she ask for the position. She hadn't thought of doing that. She prepared what she wanted to say and made an appointment with the head of human resources. They told her no but indicated they were impressed by her initiative. A few weeks later, they offered her another job with more responsibility and higher pay. She took it.

But Jerry had a different experience. When he Politely and Powerfully confronted his manager about putting him down in front of others and wanted to know why he was doing it, the man admitted that he wanted Jerry to quit.

"At first I was really upset," Jerry told me. "I regretted opening my mouth. My wife and I had just bought a new house and the economy was still pretty bad. It wasn't a great time to be worried about getting fired or looking for a job. But the confrontation motivated me to find a new job and I did. I now have a manager who treats me with respect. I'm much happier now, although it was a rough and uncertain time there for a while."

Some people may say Jerry took a risk and got paid back for it. I say, in this context, the risk was worth it. In fact, the risk led to a higher payoff for Jerry. "No" was the right answer. It got Jerry on the move. Do you want to work for someone who doesn't treat you with respect?

Even though no doesn't seem like a positive answer, I believe it's better to know where you stand than to stand in the old place feeling mistreated, misunderstood, or just plain unhappy.

Don't WAC Behind Someone's Back

If you ask someone else to WAC for you, you may avoid the confrontation, but you may end up bringing a lot of negative consequences on yourself. The home office of an insurance company had this problem:

Peter didn't like that his assistant, Kate, was often too loud when she talked. It drove him crazy when she would shout him questions or answers rather than use her intercom. Peter complained to the office manager. He wanted her to say something to Kate.

The office manager did discuss the problem with her. But Kate was upset that Peter didn't come directly to her. She didn't realize she was driving him crazy. It embarrassed her that the office manager was involved and that perhaps others in the office knew and felt the same way. Her attitude changed after that. Eventually she quit. She was a good worker not easily replaced.

The same office manager was later approached by another assistant on another issue: "Megan is using my printer. She's tying it up and I need it." The office manager told her, "You need to discuss this calmly with Megan. Does she realize you're busy and need the printer?"

"I don't really know."

"Well," she said, "find out."

The office manager realized that if she could help the people in the office work their problems out directly, people would get along better in the long run. She gave the assistant a crash course on positive confrontation. The situation was quickly resolved. No one got upset.

In this example, Peter was being a wimp. He was afraid to say something to his assistant and look what happened. In most situations it's usually better to be direct rather than to use an emissary to confront for you.

I have heard countless tales of family feuds that begin the same way. One sister tells another sister something about one of the sisters-in-law, and when the sister-in-law gets a bad vibe, she tells her husband. The husband then tries to talk to his sister. Then she gets mad and tells the other sister about the brother. The other sister calls the other brother and now the whole family is in a fight. It is usually best to deal directly with those you need to confront.

The Focus Is Still on You

Though this chapter has focused on the other person and the many ways he or she can respond to your WAC, your main focus should always remain on being Polite and Powerful. When you check in with the other person, you may find that he is only too happy to give you what you've asked for.

However, the other person may get offended by your WAC'em words. She may act rudely or even shout at you. You can't control the other person. You can only control yourself and how you react. Polite and Powerful behavior, even if you're the only one using it, will still give you the best chance for positive conflict resolution.

10

Eleven Simple Things You Can Do to Have a Positive Confrontation

'␣ve talked a lot about how to prevent a negative confrontation. When a confrontation goes bad, there are many common reasons why: negative wording, accusatory statements, bad body language. When a confrontation goes well, there are also common reasons in play. Usually it's because you went into the conversation with a solid WAC'em worked out. You paid attention to your words and nonverbal behavior. But there's even more you can do to contribute to your success. Often, when I analyze confrontations that have gone well, the person initiating the WAC'em discussion followed eleven simple steps. They really matter, and you can try them too.

1. Pick Your Conflict Wisely

Once you realize that you know how to assertively speak up and handle yourself, you decide to give WAC'em a try. But how do you recognize which situations are worth speaking up about?

Since WAC'em is a formula that can be applied to many situations, you could probably confront lots of people every day. But who wants to go through life having many confrontations, even positive ones?

Because people who are new to positive confrontation often need help getting started, I've developed five pick-your-conflict questions to provide you with a calm, nonemotional way to help you decide whether a situation is worth WACing someone.

- Does this really affect you?

  You may be tempted to think that if a situation bothers you, that means it has an effect on you. Recall Melissa, the woman who was irritated that her sister-in-law didn't cook for her husband (Melissa's brother). That situation had no direct effect on Melissa or her quality of her life, so it was not her conflict. (There may be other issues between the women, but it is not the cooking.) If you can't pinpoint how a situation has a direct effect on you, this is most likely not your confrontation to have.

- Is it your responsibility to say something?

  On the other hand, if it is your business to WAC someone and you don't, your professional image can suffer. If you are the owner, chairperson, director, or person in charge, it is usually your job to speak up if someone needs to be WAC'ed. If you're hosting a meeting or out-of-town guests and a problem arises, it is your responsibility to address it.

- Is this an ongoing situation?

  Is your situation an ongoing problem or a onetime occurrence? If the situation is ongoing, for example, your coworker keeps making negative comments about your work, you may want to speak up. But if you and the person who is bothering you are like two proverbial ships passing in the night, why bother? You're not likely to see the person who was texting while walking and bumped into you in Times Square ever again. If the bothersome behavior is an isolated incident, you may choose to ignore it. There are exceptions. Suppose you are sitting next to a man on a train and he is screaming into his cell phone. You may want to say something (or move your seat) or else you're going to have a very long trip.

- Can the person influence the outcome?

  Many times we get upset with people for situations they do not control and cannot change. We have all seen people exploding at airline ticket agents. The plane is delayed; you cannot change that and the agent cannot change that. The agent is simply the messenger, so even politely telling her that you need to get to Boston isn't going to make your plane appear. And if you are nasty to her, she may do as little as possible to get you on the next plane out.

- Is this safe or unsafe?
  As noted in Chapter 9, why would you confront someone in an unsafe situation? Let it go!

These five pick-your-conflict questions can help you decide whether or not to WAC someone. But some people may still have a difficult time, even after reviewing the questions, and that's fine too. Don't rush or make hasty decisions. You can review these questions again later, like Ashley did. Her manager was texting during their meetings. After reviewing the questions, she decided not to say anything. Yet it kept bothering her. When Ashley revisited the questions one month later, she realized that his behavior was affecting her, it was an ongoing situation, and she needed to speak up. She WAC'ed him and the discussion went well.

2. Start Small

Let me caution you—don't stop reading this book and immediately go out and WAC the "big one." The big one being your bad-tempered supervisor, your mother-in-law, or someone else whose reaction to being confronted can have a big impact on your relationship or your life. I'm not saying that you shouldn't confront this person, but I am saying it's wise to work up to the confrontations that will have the biggest impact on your life.

Not to oversimplify, but many aspects of positive confrontation become habits, like learning to drive a car safely. For most of us, it's awkward and even scary in the beginning. Yet, after lessons and practice and experience, you don't have to think about it, you just do it. Positive confrontation is the same way. It's a skill that will become more comfortable over time.

If you can't even imagine WAC'ing the "big one," slowly build your confidence and read on for more advice.

3. Practice

I hate to be like your old piano teacher, but I have to tell you to practice. We talked about writing down your WAC'em words. It's also important to practice saying them. Read your words out loud. Listen to how they sound. Are they harsh? Too weak? How would you feel if someone said those words to you? Judging how the words will come across to the other person is vitally important.

Repeat your words a number of times. You're don't want to memorize your WAC'em words. You're not going to recite a script during your confrontation. But by practicing your WAC'em wording, you'll feel more comfortable and confident speaking to the other person. You're less likely to be harsh or to discount yourself.

Role-playing with another person can also help you practice your WAC'em words and nonverbal skills. Play both roles. Try to think of the obstacles you might encounter during a difficult conversation. The more you practice, the more comfortable and confident you will be later in real life.

Finding a positive role model can also help you handle confrontations. As I mentioned at the beginning of this book, my role model for handling conflict was Ann Davis. I used to watch how she handled herself in tough situations and learned from her. If you can, choose a mentor you can watch and interact with on a regular basis. Notice this person's words and body language. Notice how he or she handles difficult situations. You don't want to copy the person word for word or gesture for gesture. Adapt what he or she says or does to fit your own style.

4. Handle Your Jitters

I'd like to give you a word of encouragement about nerves. If you worry that you'll get so nervous that all your practice will go out the window, this is normal. You're definitely not alone in having this fear. Many people feel very nervous when it comes to difficult conversations. They're afraid of making mistakes, failing, or encountering the other person's reaction.

It really is normal to be nervous. Your nervousness is just energy. Energy isn't good or bad; it's how you handle the energy that counts. Don't you think successful actors, athletes, and CEOs get nervous? Of course they do. But they are successful because they have moved ahead despite any fears they may have about making mistakes or "losing it" in front of others. They have learned how to harness their nervous energy to create a positive experience. Many people say that nervous energy even helps them perform better.

A friend of mine is a successful writer. He told me that when he has to read in front of an audience he feels like not enough air is getting into his lungs. He's convinced he's going to pass out or hyperventilate. But he doesn't. "I take a few really deep breaths before I start. By the time I'm on the third paragraph, I'm calm and having a great time. I just have to sweat it out a little in the beginning."

Fake It Until You Feel It

You know the old saying, If you look like a duck, walk like a duck, and quack like a duck, you are a duck. I call this trick "fake it until you feel it." People tell me they love this advice because it really works. If you don't look nervous, how will the other person know? She won't, unless you tell her.

A TIP FOR HANDLING THE JITTERS

It sounds obvious, but breathe. People tend to hold their breath or take shallow breaths when they're nervous. Before approaching someone for a difficult conversation, take a few deep breaths. Draw air through your nose and deeply into your abdominal cavity and keep drawing until your abdomen is fully expanded. Hold this breath for a slow count of seven. Then release your breath through your mouth, slowly as you count to eight. In two or three breaths you're going to feel better. It works.

I have reached a point in my life where I can pretty much WAC anybody Politely and Powerfully, but that doesn't mean I don't still get nervous. I do sometimes get the jitters. But now I can look back and see my successful confrontations, and that helps me move forward each time. Even when the outcome of a confrontation wasn't what I wanted, I still handled myself Politely and Powerfully, and knowing that was also important for building my confidence.

5. Visualize Yourself Being Polite and Powerful

Part of your preparation for a confrontation is mental. Visualization techniques are a powerful tool for many people. Some people swear that just by visualizing themselves playing flawless tennis they can improve their game. A very fit looking woman told me that when she was on a diet, she would visualize herself in a pair of size 6 jeans and that helped her stay on track.

Tom, a quality assurance engineer for an aerospace corporation, described his dramatic fantasies of "telling off" the people in his department who were giving him a "hard time"—not getting reports to him on time. "In my mind, I would confront these three specific people in my department. I would get very righteous, yell, and of course have the perfect comeback. Even just thinking about it could get my heart pumping and adrenaline flowing."

These fantasies were not helpful. Nothing changed. Tom didn't confront anyone and only got more upset. After he learned the power of positive confrontation, Tom decided to put his fantasy life to work for him in a positive way. "I would picture standing up straight with my face looking relaxed and calm. I would practice my WAC'em wording and say, 'When I don't get your papers on time, my part of the project gets sidetracked. I need to get them on time. Is there any reason why this can't happen?'

"When I finally did it, I was nervous but I managed to say everything I wanted to say, politely and powerfully. They apologized. I get the papers on time. It was pretty easy."

When you get upset about someone's behavior, try to calm down. Visualize yourself as the Polite and Powerful person you are. Like Tom, picture yourself confronting the person using your WAC words and being calm and self-assured.

6. Use Affirmations

Before every seminar, I tell myself, "I can do it. I can handle it."

These simple statements are my affirmations. Even after all of these years, saying them in my head before a seminar or presentation is still a part of my mental preparation.

When you're about to have a confrontation remind yourself, "I can do it" or "I can handle it." "I am a Polite and Powerful person."

I know it sounds corny, but try using affirmations; they really do work. Your subconscious believes whatever you tell it. If you tell it you're a wimp, you're a wimp. But if you tell it positive things about your ability to handle conflict, you are more likely to be Polite and Powerful. These statements will get into your mental loop—that string of statements we whisper to ourselves continually—and they will have a positive effect on you.

People think this touchy-feely kind of thing can't possibly work. It sounds too simple to be that powerful. I challenge the naysayers to try it for a few weeks and then tell me it doesn't work.

Andrew tried it. He is a very bright mechanical engineer who told me he used to stand at the bus stop going to a job he didn't like and say to himself, "But I can't get another job. I'm stuck. I would have to get a new degree. That would take too long. No one will hire me."

These negative statements were in Andrew's loop. He tuned in, decided he didn't like what he was telling himself, and decided to tell himself something new. "I stood there and told myself over and over again that I could get another job that I liked better. I could do it. I would get the skills."

Andrew did get the job and the skills, and you can do it too. Check in and listen to what you're saying to yourself. You may be surprised to find out what you're thinking. If necessary, reprogram a negative loop with positive statements. Keep it simple; a short "I" statement will do. Use present tense verbs: "I can, I will, I know." Keep the message positive. "I won't mess up the WAC" is not positive. "I can handle this confrontation" is positive.

7. Pick the Right Time and Place

You've prepared. You've practiced. You've visualized and affirmed. You're ready to roll. It's time to hunt the other person down and do this WAC'em thing and get it done. Ready or not, here I come!

Please don't take this hit-him-over-the-head approach.

In your excitement or desire to "get it over with," don't force a confrontation to happen at the wrong time. Privacy is very important when WAC'ing another person. Right after a meeting, while other people are lingering about, is not a good time to confront someone. It may be a good time to ask the person if he's available to talk later in private.

If you don't have this kind of access to the person or opportunity, make it happen. Email, phone, or text and request a meeting. If you happen to run into the person and she is alone, you still need to ask, "Is this a good time for you to talk?" or "Do you have a few minutes? There's something I'd like to talk to you about." The person may not have time to talk. She may be heading off to a meeting or leaving to pick up a child from school.

Just because you run into the person and no one else is around doesn't mean you should confront the person right then and there. You may be in a noisy or distracting location. You may not be in the right frame of mind to be Polite and Powerful. I'm not saying that you must have ideal conditions, but as a guideline, if you're not calm, it's easy to lose control. If you're not calm, it is usually best to postpone the conversation. If the other person doesn't seem calm, postpone it. If you know the other person is dealing with a stressful situation, such as a sick loved one or a looming deadline, you should probably wait on your WAC.

If you don't want to be alone with the person because, say, she has a reputation for losing her temper, arrange to meet in a public place. Most office buildings have a coffee shop on the premises or nearby. Meet during working hours when you are certain others will be around.

8. Don't Drink Before or During

I caution you about having difficult conversations in bars. Having a drink may help you relax, but it's also an opportunity for confrontations to get out of hand or sidetracked.

After a few drinks, you may talk too much and say something you later regret. You may end up hugging, but chances are the next day, you both might feel embarrassed. You may not remember or have a clear understanding of what was said or agreed to. You probably won't have accomplished anything. Alcohol and WAC'em don't mix.

9. Keep It Short and Simple

Some people talk too much in tense situations. Women especially tend to explain and explain and then explain some more. Nervousness often causes you to keep talking. Relief can also cause you to talk too much.

Once you have checked in with the other person and are satisfied with the outcome, don't keep talking. You might undo your WAC'em words. Use an exit line and move on:

> I appreciate your time. I have a meeting to get to now.
> Thanks for listening. I'll talk to you later.
> I have a phone call to make, so let's leave it at that.

Also, limit your discussion to one issue at a time. This will help you keep it short and simple, and you won't get sidetracked.

10. Follow Up

The person you confronted might have wonderful intentions of doing what you asked. When you did your WAC'em and checked in, the person may have said, "Sure, no problem." But people don't change overnight. Sometimes you are dealing with people's bad habits. It may be necessary to reinforce your point at a later time. It may be necessary to give the person a little time and space to make the changes you asked for. A follow-up to check-in may sound something like this:

> Remember yesterday, when I mentioned that your music was
>   too loud?
> This is what I meant by that discussion we had.
> You wanted me to point out when you were doing that. Well
>   you're doing that!

It would be wonderful if you could WAC'em once and be done, but that doesn't always happen. Schedule a follow-up meeting if necessary. Review any agreements that were made. Make adjustments if needed. At work, you may want to follow up in writing.

Even if you were right and the other person was wrong, Polite and Powerful people don't gloat over their victory. They congratulate themselves in silence. They don't need to be right. Powerful people aren't powerful because they get their way. They are powerful because they have the confidence to be gracious. If the person you confronted makes the changes you've asked for, thank him. Again, keep it simple:

"I appreciate that you signed me up for the class. The training was very helpful."

Or

"Thank-you for getting the report to me on time. It really helped."

11. Learn from Your Experiences

First, feel good about yourself. No matter what the outcome, you tried to have a positive confrontation. Next, evaluate the experience. Ask yourself these questions:

- What did I learn from the experience?

- How can I improve next time?

If you're not successful, don't beat yourself up. It doesn't help. You are practicing new skills and mastering them will take time. It's okay to not like how you handled a situation and still like yourself. If you keep saying "I'm stupid" or "I blew it again," these negative statements will end up in your loop and you will be stuck in a negative frame of mind.

> Think about a person you confronted in your past. What was the issue and how did you resolve it? Would you do it differently now? How so?

Keep a WAC'em Diary

Many people new to positive confrontation find it helpful to keep a WAC'em diary. Start by answering the following:

- What was the reason for the encounter?

- What was your WAC'em?

- Where were you?

- Did you have privacy?

- How was your body language?

- What did the other person say?

- Did you give the other person a chance to talk?

- How was it resolved?

- If you choose to confront the other person again, what will you say? If you could do it again, what would you do differently?

After four or five encounters look back over the pages. This is an easy way to identify any similar kinds of problems you may be having:

- Are you having difficulty with the same person?

- Are you having the same or related kinds of conflicts again and again?

- Are conflicts occurring at any particular time or place?

- Do you have more conflicts at home or work?

- What skills do you need to practice?

You will only need to do this until you get used to confronting Politely and Powerfully.

I can assure you, positive confrontation gets easier. It also gets more rewarding. When you WAC instead of attack, the benefits you enjoy are numerous. When you begin to experience these benefits, having confrontations isn't nearly as hard. You've got lots of incentive to continue on the Polite and Powerful path.

11

WAC'em in Writing

So far, we've talked about how to deliver your WAC'em words in the context of a face-to-face discussion. I have encouraged you to write down your W and your A, to help you clarify your thoughts and come up with positive wording. But what about WAC'ing someone via email? Or even a letter? Can this be an effective way to resolve a conflict, especially if you're terribly nervous about having the difficult conversation?

Email may seem like a tempting option. If you must deny someone a promotion because of poor performance, why not break the news via email? You won't have to see his face crumple.

If you want to WAC your manager for excluding you from a meeting, you don't have to be there when she sighs heavily or, worse, makes you feel grateful for even having a job. What college student wouldn't rather explain why her paper will be late via email rather than have to sit in her professor's office, feeling the sweat trickle down her face?

It's very tempting to have confrontations or to deliver bad news in writing. But you need to think carefully about WAC'ing electronically before you choose this option. I am not saying that writing can't *sometimes* be a valid WAC'em delivery method; however, you need to make sure you're choosing this option for the right reasons.

First, let me clarify why face-to-face discussions are usually the best option for a Polite and Powerful confrontation. (I said best option, not easiest option.) When you WAC a person in person, you have four advantages.

1. You Know the Person Has Been WAC'ed

The person may or may not be receptive to your WAC in a face-to-face meeting, but at least you know you had the conversation. If you send an email, you can't be sure the person received it or read it. Or whether she understands what's bothering you and what you're asking for. Some of my clients get literally hundreds of emails a day, so your message could easily get overlooked or end up in the spam folder. You may save yourself the anxiety and nervousness of having to WAC in person, but you now have a new kind of anxiety. Did he get the email or not? Is she mad at me now? Surely he would have answered me by now? Should I send another email? Should I call?

What About "Read Receipt" Requests?

Yes, there is a "read receipt" request that you may be able to send with your email, but I don't advise it. This is an email notification feature that is delivered to you when a recipient opens (and presumably reads) an email you send. This receipt confirms that the recipient has at least seen your message and records the time. However, you still can't be 100 percent sure the person has read it. Furthermore, some networks automatically block these requests and people often turn the feature off.

2. You Have Nonverbal Signals to Soften Your Message

If you're worried that your words may sound harsh or the person may not be able to handle being WAC'ed, your nonverbals can help your delivery. You can express your concern for the person's feelings by the look on your face, by the openness of your body language, and a gentle tone of voice.

You can also see the other person's nonverbal reaction, which will clue you in about how your WAC is being received. Is the person looking at you? What about her facial expression? Has he crossed his arms in defensiveness?

You simply don't have the benefit of nonverbal messages in electronic communication.

What About Emoticons?

Sorry ☹, but an emoticon cannot equal a real person in expressing regret. Though an emoticon can occasionally help soften your words or express a shared feeling with someone you know well, I don't recommend using these symbols if you're WAC'ing via email. They might undo the seriousness of your words, or overdo it: "The comment you made in the meeting was inappropriate ☹. Please don't criticize me in front of the team. If you have concerns please come to me in private. ☺"

Though you might like them and may have downloaded dozens of them to insert into your electronic communication, many people dislike them or don't understand them. A friend didn't know that the symbol >:(indicates anger. For these reasons, I caution you from using emoticons while WACing someone and for professional communications.

3. You Know Where You Stand—Instantly

When you check in and ask "can you do this?" You get a real-time answer and you know the person's opinion about what you've asked for. This immediate response can help you resolve the conflict quickly.

4. You're Trying to Be a Polite and Powerful Person

If the person you're confronting is someone you see regularly, when she reads your email, she may say to herself, "This is ridiculous. Why didn't he just tell me? Why do I have to read about it?"

Others may see you as wimpy if you don't speak with them face-to-face. This is especially true for WAC'ing people you work with professionally. A confident, poised, and ultimately promotable person is one who is viewed as being able to Politely and Powerfully handle difficult situations, including face-to-face confrontations.

As well as questioning your confidence, the other person may wonder, "Is he afraid of me?" or "Do I seem unapproachable?"

You'll further damage your image and your WAC if you start your email with an apology: "I'm sorry for writing this but I usually get so emotional when I try to talk about these kinds of things." If you have to apologize for writing, should you be emailing the WAC in the first place?

Remember how easy it is to talk on and on when you're nervous? The same is true for writing an email. You may be tempted to over-explain and then explain a little more. "Oh just one more little thing that's bothering me . . . " You lose your clarity if you're wordy.

When It's Okay to WAC'em in Writing

There are some positives to WAC'ing a person in writing. The following concerns may justify WAC'ing someone in writing:

1. Aggression. If you think the person will become aggressive and you won't be able to express yourself clearly, WACing in writing may be preferable. This doesn't mean the person will read your email or letter and not react badly, but you will have a better chance of getting your point across.

2. Complexity. If there is a complex or serious issue between you and the other person, you may want to explain it in writing. When you put your WAC'em in writing, you can be sure of your words. As long as you edit yourself, nothing is going to slip out and cause a problem as it could in conversation.

A wife WAC'ed her husband by writing him a letter. She explained all the ways his flip comments put her down. She discussed how it affected her self-esteem and how crucial it was to their marriage for the comments to stop. She had a lot to say and wanted to be clear about her wording, so writing a letter was a good choice for her. Her husband read the letter and stopped putting her down. She's now able to WAC him in person.

When you write, the words are permanent. That is the good and bad news about writing your WAC'em. It's good news because it allows the person to read your words and then read them again, if necessary. The person can take the time to really try to understand your concern.

It's bad news because your words are now permanent, contained in an email, and easily forwarded and shared with others. You can't ever deny what you wrote and you can't take it back.

3. Avoidance. If the person uses humor, interrupts you, or walks on a treadmill while you talk, an email or a letter will allow you to get your thoughts out without interruption or distraction. I have a friend who told me she couldn't WAC her father because he always made jokes to avoid getting into serious discussions. And to make matters worse, he was funny. She would end up laughing during the talks, but still frustrated. She said she tried to bring him back to the issue by saying, "Dad, you're so funny, but when you make jokes out of the serious things I'm trying to tell you, I feel bad." That still didn't work. So she wrote him a letter because he didn't regularly use his email account.

4. Distance. If geography makes it impossible to say your WAC'em words in person, go ahead and put your thoughts in writing. Anna's father-in-law exploded at her during her family's annual holiday visit after her young child broke something in his house. They cut the visit short, but when she returned home, she was still upset. Anna decided to WAC him in a letter because he lived far away, didn't use email regularly, and the writing would allow her to say exactly what she wanted to say. She wrote that it was important for him to remain in her life and yet she wouldn't allow him to explode at her. Anna told him that in the future, she wanted to hear his concerns, but she didn't want him screaming at her.

Good Old-Fashioned Letters

I tell people yes, email is a convenient form of writing, and just about everyone has email, but don't give up on letters. Even though letters aren't used as often in our day-to-day communication, there are benefits. As the examples above illustrate, some people don't use email regularly. Even college-age students don't check their email as often as you might think, as my friend discovered when she WAC'ed her son in an email. She ended with: "Please contact me as soon as you read this." She was waiting and waiting . . . finally she called him and asked, "Why didn't you answer my email?" He responded, "What email?" For teens and young adults, texting and social media are often the preferred forms of communication.

But for others, sending a letter can be a more formal and thoughtful form of communication. A letter is also a more private form of communication. You can't easily forward a letter you receive via snail mail. Sure, you can show it to someone, scan and copy it, but an email can be sent to hundreds of people in an instant.

Writing and sending a letter is a more time-consuming process. You write or type it, print it, put it in an envelope, get a stamp, and mail it. Therefore, you have plenty of time to write your WAC'em words, edit them, and if you're angry, to calm down. We all know how easy it is to dash off an email in anger. Many of us have done it at one time or another. And then there are the true nightmare email scenarios we have all heard about.

Email Horror Stories

I saw a cartoon of a man rushing out of a time machine yelling to his earlier self, who was sitting at the computer, "Don't hit send!"

I know many people who wish they could get into that time machine and do the same. An HR manager once told me that he WAC'ed his co-worker via email. The recipient didn't like being WAC'ed and, to even the score, forwarded his message all over the company and beyond.

Plus, and this is especially true if you're dashing off an email in anger, you can unwittingly send it to the wrong person. I heard a story about a magazine editor who was very upset with his publisher. He wrote a nasty email about her to his coworker. He said that as he hit the send button, he had the terrible realization that it was the publisher's address on the screen. The worst part was he could see her in her office. He heard the little ding indicating she had mail. He saw her hear it and turn to her computer. He left his job that day.

As a general guideline, don't send emails when you're angry or upset. A friend of mine, when she is upset, writes any email in a Word document first. This helps her calm down by adding extra steps before the communication can be sent. Also, don't load the address into the message until you are calm and ready to send. You can't accidentally send an email if it has no address.

Writing Suggestions for WAC'em

If you do write to someone about a bothersome situation or concern, the quality of your writing becomes important. I went into a regional bank office to teach business writing shortly after a vice president sent an email to all employees trying to reassure them that the company would work with them during an upcoming transit strike. His suggestions were good ones. Unfortunately his wording was negative. Among other things, he wrote, "We will work with you, but we don't want any of you abusing the system."

Not only did the employees begrudge him; they begrudged the company as well.

Read on for Polite and Powerful writing guidelines:

1. WAC'em applies. In writing, your W is the same as for face-to-face conversations. You tell the person what's bothering you. The A is the same too. You tell the person what you want. The C will be the slightly different. You need to ask the person to get back to you. At work, you can include a request, "A response by the end of the week," or, depending on the situation, "Please give this some thought. I'll be back in town next week and we can talk." Or indicate that you'll give the person a call and let him know when.

2. Choose your words carefully. Go back to Chapter 7 and review the suggestions for wording your WAC. They apply to your writing also. Pay attention to some key points. Be polite. Eliminate harsh or negative words. No name calling or cursing. Positive wording is always critical. If you write, "Any reasonable person would conclude . . . " you imply that the reader is *not* a reasonable person. "You failed to . . . " blames the other person. These statements would sound harsh in person and appear even harsher in writing.

3. Write the way you speak. Even though email is a more informal way to communicate, people have a tendency to become formal when WAC'ing this way. Remember, you want to create a conversational tone. You want to connect with the person, especially when you're not face-to-face. You don't use words like "herewith" or "heretofore," so why write that way? Besides, most people don't know what these words mean. (One participant joked and said heretofore means "we're here in your class till four.")

How many times have you ever said, "Pursuant to our conversation . . . " or "It has become necessary to reiterate that your excessive tardiness . . . "? You would never say these things, so why write them?

4. Appearance matters. When using email, you must ensure that it can be read easily from the screen.

- Use at least a 10 or 12 point font that is large enough for people to see.

- Long blocks of text can seem daunting. Keep paragraphs short and double-space between them to enhance readability.

- Keep bold and underline to a minimum. Convey your WAC'em through your words. *IF YOU USE EMPHASIS TECHNIQUES, LIKE THIS ONE, IT'S LIKE SHOUTING!* People are insulted by this—and who can blame them?

- Use punctuation to punctuate, not to create an effect. Again, use clarity to get your points across, not formatting tricks. One exclamation mark and one question mark only. Do not do this!!!!!!!!!! One woman wrote an email to her employees in bold 36 point type: "The meeting is Monday. Everyone must attend!!!!!!!!!!!!" (Her group was insulted. They understood perfectly what "everyone," "must," and "attend" meant.)

- If you're going to mail a letter, use decent paper. No Post-it note collages and no scraps of paper. Don't tear pages out of a spiral notebook and leave the fringe on. Plain white paper or personal stationery is fine.

5. Use a salutation and closing. By its design, an email is a memo, and technically, unlike a letter, does not require a salutation. However, we have adapted some standard rules of letter writing to email writing. We know, either consciously or not, that when we use a salutation to start an email, we seem less abrupt and more friendly, which is helpful when you're WAC'ing. Using Dear _____ (more formal) or Hi _____(less formal but still professional) can set a friendly tone.

Some additional guidelines:

- Don't use nicknames without permission. I don't like it when people call me Barb. I know a man named Michael who often discards emails or letters addressed "Dear Mike."

- Don't address someone as "Dear Paul" if you always call him "Mr. Bennett."

- Drop the salutation if you are conversing back and forth with someone.

- Include a closing. In a business or professional situation, when you use a salutation, you need to include a closing in your email. You can use "Thanks," "Regards," "Best regards," or "Sincerely." If it's someone you know well, however, you can sometimes skip the closing. Simply use your C as your closing: "I'm looking forward to speaking with you." Or "I look forward to continuing this discussion with you." Or "Let me know when it's a good time to talk."

- Make sure your signature block includes your full name, a telephone number and extension, a mailing address if appropriate, and your email address.

6. Write a draft. If you're very frustrated or upset with the other person, the first draft you write is the one you shouldn't send. Do what my friend does: open a blank document—outside of your email—and go wild. Spill your guts and blow off steam. After you have vented your frustration, take a deep breath and edit what you wrote. Even if you're not emotional, it's still a good idea to write a draft or two. Be careful not to over-explain. Say what you need to say and then stop writing.

Most professional writers understand that a few, if not several, drafts are required to capture what you really want to say.

7. Proofread and read aloud. You are almost ready to mail the letter or send the email. But before you do, there is one more crucial step: print the draft and proofread it. Catching mistakes is much harder when you are reading from a screen. And reading your words aloud is a good acid test for how you message sounds. If your words sound harsh to you, chances are the other person will think so too. Go back and eliminate the negativity. Typos or missing words can also contribute to misunderstandings. A customer service representative wrote a letter to a customer in response to a billing dispute: "Unfortunately we are going to credit you $700." He meant to write, "We are *not* going to credit you $700." But they had to pay her . . . she had it in writing.

8. Give it some time. Never hit send or take a paper that's still warm from your hands or the printer and then run out and mail it. You need a cooling off period. Emails especially are too easy to dash off and too easy to send. One click and it lives forever.

Keep the email in your draft folder or put the letter aside for a little while, and then reread it. If you are sure that the email or letter says what you want it to say, Politely and Powerfully, then you can hit send or drop it in the mail. (*See box on facing page.*)

One Last Suggestion for Emailing

Be careful if emailing from your smartphone. You may want to wait until you're back at your computer and can write carefully and without distraction. One woman emailed her thank-you note after a job interview from her phone, but forgot it was an email and used text shortcuts. She told me she didn't get the job as a result.

Texting and IM Are Not Good Ways to WAC

Texting and instant messaging (IM) are very casual and very brief and most often don't work for WAC'em. People typically put less time and thought into them than email. These communications are often dashed off—and you don't want to be rushing when you WAC. It requires careful thought.

EXCERPT FROM A
REAL-LIFE WAC'EM LETTER

Cynthia is a student in a creative writing program. She became upset with her writing professor for using what she considered harsh language in her critiques. Since they primarily communicated online, Cynthia felt comfortable WAC'ing her via email:

Dear Marie,

The writing workshop has been such a great experience. I believe I can truly improve my writing by working with you. Please understand, however, that when you use words such as silly, ridiculous, and boring to critique my work, it makes it difficult for me to hear and apply your otherwise constructive criticism. I would appreciate it if you would bear this in mind in our future work together.

Please let me know your thoughts on this.

Result:
Cynthia's professor wrote back: "I'm so glad you told me about this. I had no idea I was being so negative."

That said, I know a woman who WAC'ed her coworker via text and they were sitting in the same space, literally with their backs to each other. "Jamie told me you told her about my interview. I really need for you to keep it secret. Thanks." In this case the sender did not want to get into the fact that she had asked her coworker not to tell anyone. She felt it most important to quickly reinforce her wish to keep the interview secret. Later after work, her coworker apologized.

To WAC in Writing or Not?

Ultimately, bearing in mind what we have just considered, you will need to judge each situation on its own and decide whether or not writing an email or letter is an effective way to approach the other person. For the most part, my advice is to WAC the other person in person whenever possible. But if you decide that email is appropriate, take the same care in preparing your WAC'em words as you would if delivering them in person.

12

WAC'ing by Phone

Face-to-face discussions or emails are not the only ways to WAC. Many people ask me if WAC'ing by phone is the next best thing to an in-person discussion.

Again, it depends.

The woman described in Chapter 11 who WAC'ed her father-in-law in a letter knew she had the phone as an option but feared his temper. She was new to positive confrontation and was nervous. She was afraid she wouldn't be able to get her words out correctly. In her case, writing the letter was a good interim step. She may have laid the groundwork for future conversations on the phone or in person.

Sometimes you'll want to have a phone discussion because you know you won't be seeing that person for a while.

Other times the WAC'em just happens. You're on the phone with your friend when the issue bothering you just comes up. You have been thinking about saying something and you have been preparing your WAC'em words. You are ready to say something. Why wait? Perfect opportunity.

Many of the same advantages and disadvantages to WAC'em in writing apply to WAC'em over the phone. On the plus side, it is more direct and personal because you are speaking with the person. A real-time discussion can occur.

On the Down Side

- You can't use body language to show openness or concern.

- It can be too easy to reach someone. Many people carry their phones with them all the time and are always available. You may end up having the discussion before you have your WAC prepared.

- You can't be sure you're reaching someone at a favorable time. Some of us answer our phones in less than ideal locations (movies, restrooms, restaurant tables, etc.). A person may be busy with company or about to go into a meeting.

- The person can make up excuses to avoid the conversation. It's much harder to refuse to speak to someone when you're face-to-face. However, over the phone the "I have company" or "I'm about to go into a meeting" statements can be excuses for hanging up.

- It can be hard to hear over a cell phone. If the person you're trying to speak with is walking and talking outside, you may have a hard time hearing. There could be all kinds of background noise.

- He or she can hang up on you—accidentally or on purpose. Granted, a person can storm off during a face-to-face conversation, but you can't know for sure if you're being hung up on. The call could have been dropped, especially if the person is moving around while speaking with you.

When WAC'ing by Phone . . .

In Chapter 11, I talked about the reasons why it might be helpful to WAC in writing and those reasons apply to the phone as well. But if you decide to WAC using the phone, here are some additional tips for handling the conversation:

- Ask the person, "Are you somewhere you can talk for a few minutes?" or "Is this a good time to talk?" If you and the person text regularly, you can send a text asking to talk, but don't text anything more than that. You could scare the person, or get her defenses up, if you say something like (and I'm translating from text speak), "I really need to speak with you now! It's very, very important. I'm upset about something; can you talk?"

- Ask if would be better to call on another number or perhaps a landline, which often has better reception.

- Try to set up your talk in advance or let the person know you'll be calling. This will help ensure you're reaching someone at a good time.

- Watch the tone and volume of your voice. The only nonverbal that you can use to help make the conversation Polite and Powerful will be your tone of voice, so make sure you control it. Many people have a tendency to shout more on their mobile phones than they do on landlines, often without realizing it.

Don't WAC by Voice Mail

You may be asking, Who would WAC in a voice message? Yet I have heard many stories of this happening. Usually it doesn't work. People often play their messages on speaker phone, and you don't know who might hear what you're saying. Also, if you say something you regret, the other person will have a recording of it. Keep in mind, angry voice mail messages can go viral.

A WAC should not be left on someone's voice mail, not even a calm one: "Carl, your presentation contained numerous mistakes and I was embarrassed in front of our new team members. I need you to be more careful and proofread your PowerPoint. Please assure me this won't happen again. Thanks."

This could have been a good WAC—in person. When Carl returned from lunch and heard the message, he became upset. While his presentation did include mistakes, he still had the right to offer an explanation, or at least a context, for why they happened. (It was a rushed project, he received many of the slides with errors in them at the last minute, he had gotten bumped from his flight and was on the red eye and arrived just in time for the meeting.) Carl was able to explain everything. He owned the mistakes and assured his manager they would never happen again, but until he had an opportunity to talk, he was upset.

Tips for Voice Mail Messages

- Don't leave ominous messages: "Kate, you're really in trouble this time. I need to talk to you ASAP." Kate will be looking forward to calling you back like she's looking forward to getting a cavity filled. Even "we need to talk" sounds ominous. My son said this on a voice mail to me and I called him in a bit of a panic. "What's wrong?" I asked. "Nothing," he replied. "It's just been a while since we've talked."

- Keep it simple and positive: "Hi Beth, this is Casey. Please give me a call back when you get a chance/when you get this message."

- Don't assume the person has gotten your voice mail. Messages can get erased or lost inadvertently.

After having a phone conversation, you still need to follow up with the person. (Those guidelines were explained in Chapter 10.)

13

Handling Online Conflict

There was a time when people fought about using the landline. Growing up with two sisters, I had some epic face-to-face battles over whose turn it was to use the telephone in our house.

Though that situation may seem quaint now in the age of the personal smartphone, it's important to remember that new advances in communications technology usually come with a learning curve. Remember how most people really did need to be reminded to turn their phones off before the movie started? Now, many of us don't need the reminder to put our phones on vibrate. We have learned that if you're the person whose phone goes off during the meeting, funeral, class, or recital, you feel like a jerk.

That same learning curve applies to the online social media sites we're now using. As new social media sites and applications appear and give us more ways to interact and communicate electronically, it takes time for people to adapt and learn from their mistakes.

It also takes time for early adopters and etiquette experts to weigh in and establish guidelines for best practices. As a result, anywhere people post about their daily lives and their opinions, the opportunity for conflict can ensue.

As Clare told me, she learned the hard way that posting about political or other controversial topics on sites like Facebook can lead to problems. She posted what she thought was a harmless commentary in response to one of the many headlines during the last election. Because she only comments on posts she agrees with politically and never posts negative things to anyone in her network, she didn't expect any negative feedback.

So the next morning she was very surprised to see a hostile comment from someone in her extended family she didn't even know very well: "People like you are ruining this country." Offended, she posted back, "You are narrow-minded."

He then posted back more hostile comments. After a futile back-and-forth, with other family members now emailing her about the argument, she finally deleted his comments and unfriended him and thought that was the end of it.

But it wasn't the end. He was upset that she unfriended him and called her. An awkward conversation ensued, until she finally ended it by saying, "We will have to agree to disagree."

As you engage with people you know on social media, bear in mind that people are not always the same online as they are offline. People you like in person may annoy you online. Who knew that your coworker Casey likes to post Winston Churchill quotes every day? You never would have guessed that your friend Nick would use Twitter to share pictures of almost every meal he eats in a restaurant. Then there's your favorite niece who seems to be quite fond of taking pictures of her own face and posting them on Instagram. Welcome to the world of spammers, selfies, hash tag abusers, TMIers, boasters, pontificators, and dozens of other annoying social media users. And then there are the trolls—the people who go on social media sites, blogs, and websites with the express purpose of causing trouble and controversy with their commentary.

Why Conflict Online Is Common

While there is a learning curve for social media and eventually most people adapt to the norms, there's no guarantee that your niece will stop posting selfies anytime soon. Some people purposefully defy online social norms even as they become aware of them. As my neighbor said, "I don't care if people think I post too many pictures of my children. I do. I admit it. They don't have to look at them." And while seasoned users often adapt to best practices, just as many new people sign up and aren't aware of them.

Here are some factors that contribute to, and encourage, online conflict:

- *Lack of body language.* As you already know, your voice and non-verbals help you express yourself clearly when you're communicating face-to-face or on the phone.

- *Large online communities.* We're communicating with large numbers of people online. When it comes to having two hundred or three hundred friends or two thousand followers, and some people have many more of both, you are bound to have many people in your network you don't know well, don't know at all, and you will not agree with them on all kinds of issues.

- *Lack of restraint.* People tend to be uninhibited and outspoken when communicating online. Not being seen and not being able to see other people's reactions can dehumanize the interaction. You may say and do things online that you wouldn't in person. This is especially true when communicating anonymously under some vague screen name, like Josiegirlbooklover95. Also, someone you argue with online but don't know may be a troll who is trying to make you angry and cause conflict.

- *Entitlement.* People feel entitled to give their opinion. You don't have to wait to be asked what you think; anyone can jump in and become part of the conversation. I recently saw a Twitter drama unfold when a famous singer made a negative comment about a reality TV celebrity. The singer was then chided by one of her fans for the bad behavior. The fan was actually using polite language, even when the singer started losing her temper and tweeting what can be translated as, "Shut up and mind your own business." I couldn't help but wonder why is this "fan," who doesn't know either of these women, commenting at all? And doesn't the singer realize that if she's tweeting negative comments about someone else, she's causing conflict and making her opinions other people's business?

- *Online "silence" is unnerving.* People's involvement with social media varies. If I invite someone to join my LinkedIn or Facebook networks and my invitation is not accepted for days or even weeks, I may wonder if the person dislikes me or is snubbing me. Or if I tweet, text, post on someone's wall, poke, message, or tag her, and she does nothing in return, I am left to ponder what her online silence means, if anything. Lisa became put off when her new friend in the neighborhood women's club, Caren, didn't reply to her texts or Facebook posts. Lisa worried that Caren didn't like her or somehow had been offended, until another mom in the group clued her in: "Caren never texts anyone back and she's hardly ever on Facebook."

- *Instant reactions.* Nearly instantaneous communication lends itself to quick reactions. Even email seems slow compared with IM, texting, tweeting, and posting on Facebook and Instagram. Sometimes we need that cooling-off period to slow down and think about what we want to say and how to say it, Politely and Powerfully. Responding when we're annoyed, angry, or offended, we are more likely to pick harsh words and send emotionally charged communications: "Seriously? That's just so wrong." "I can't believe you think that." Or "how can you be so clueless?" These kinds of comments engender predictable responses: "You don't know what you're talking about." "Mind your own business." "I'm entitled to my opinion."

- *Polite disagreement is not encouraged.* There's a "like" button but no "I see it differently" button or "I disagree." Therefore, if someone posts something that offends you to a degree that you can't let it go, you can only respond with words. As I said above, when we're angry, annoyed, or upset it's easy to choose harsh words instead of calm and polite words like, "I see it differently and here's why . . . "

- *24/7 access.* Going online is second nature to people now. Normally, when we're in a bad mood, we tend to avoid people, or people can read our mood from our body language: "Jayson needs some space right now." But online, you may be in a bad mood, may have had a long day at work, may be stressed out or may have had too much to drink, and you're actively communicating with others.

- *Privacy "meters" vary.* You say private, I say post it! I can guarantee you I will never post of picture of myself in a bathing suit anywhere on the Internet, but some people are open books. The younger the online communicator, often the less inhibited, but people in their thirties and forties can also over-share or make assumptions about other people's comfort levels. When Libby shared the news to a few of her close friends (in person) that she had breast cancer, she never dreamed that one of them would comment about it on Facebook, but it happened.

Q. Should you WAC someone who refuses your friend/ follow request?
A. People refuse these requests for many reasons. They may be decluttering their network or trying to keep their private and work lives separate. Your request may have been deleted by accident, or the person may not realize who you are if you've just met, gotten married and changed your name, or if it's been thirty years since high school. If the person is someone you know well and her refusal is bothering you, you may want to ask, "I sent you a friend request and I haven't heard back from you. I'm concerned. Is everything okay? Please let me know." You are taking a risk and putting the person on the spot. What you're asking for in this situation is an explanation, which may put the person in an awkward position.

I keep waiting for the learning curve to finally catch up to well-known people, including journalists and commentators, who post or tweet comments that end up causing outrage and uproar. If you're going to tweet to thousands of followers, don't make remarks that are offensive, racist, or sexist. Humor can often be misinterpreted. People say, "I was only joking," but if it's an insulting comment, it doesn't matter what you intended; you still look bad.

Nowadays, even noncelebs can get into trouble for what they tweet, blog, and post. The learning curve still hasn't caught up to the many bloggers who are getting into conflicts with their employers. In 2005 a company fired twenty-seven workers for posting inappropriate comments on MySpace, and yet people are still getting into trouble for what they're "saying" online. Like the teacher who made headlines for writing a blog about how rude and "ratlike" some of her students are. Recently I read about a man who was reported to his company's human resources department after antibullying activists exposed him as an online bully who was tweeting from his work computer.

To Avoid Flameouts and Fails When Communicating Online

1. Err on the side of caution. If you're unsure about whether something might be offensive or inappropriate, even if it's meant to be humorous, *don't put it out there.* Also, understand that what you do put out there doesn't go away. It can, and often does, come back to haunt you. When you are being considered for a job, you will be googled, and your online social media activity will be scrutinized. If a potential employer sees that you tweeted negative comments about your last employer, posted an off-color joke on Facebook, or sees you on Instagram with a keg hose in your mouth, you have to ask yourself, Will they still want to hire me?

2. Self-assess *before* you post something controversial. When people are face-to-face, they often argue about politics, religion, and social issues. When they are online, people often argue about politics, religion, and social issues. So, if you're posting about a hot button issue or something you know is controversial, for example, your support for raising the debt ceiling, or the best candidate in an upcoming election, you should first ask yourself, What's my motive? What do I want to accomplish by sharing my opinion?

If you are reacting to a new development, especially one you disagree with, such as a court decision or some headline, you may need to give yourself a cooling-off period. Blowing off steam on social media by using inflammatory and harsh language, like "such and such politician is a total moron," is likely to create more steam. People may respond back in kind: "No, buddy, you're the moron."

3. Phrase your commentary politely. If you decide to post something controversial because you feel strongly about an issue or a candidate and you want to share how you feel or inspire others, then do so politely. Take some time to think about how you want to word your thoughts. Open a Word document and craft your thoughts cautiously. You might want to phrase your words like this: "I do not believe _____ is a good direction for our country, because_____." Or "I may be in the minority here, but it's my opinion that _____." Polite comments are likely to beget polite responses. If you post, "How can Americans be so dumb?" you might not mean any harm, but you are calling anyone who doesn't agree with you dumb. People don't like to be called dumb.

Even if you phrase your opinion or belief respectfully, others *will* respond to you, and just because you are polite and respectful does not mean everyone else will respond in kind.

How to Handle Online Conflict When It Arises

People often ask me if it's possible to successfully WAC someone online. This is a tough one to answer. In theory, yes, you can WAC someone by posting or tweeting a Polite and Powerful statement: "I don't like the implication that because we don't agree, I'm a moron. Please stop, okay?"

The downside is that an online WAC may have none of the positive elements included in a conversation, email, or phone WAC: you have determined the WAC is worthwhile because you have a relationship with the person or the situation is ongoing. You may not have written your WAC down and practiced it, and you may not be in a private communication. Online conflicts erupt quickly, are not private, and may or may not involve a person who is important to you. They can quickly spiral out of control, leaving little time to think your WAC through. You can end a face-to-face WAC by leaving a room or hanging up a phone, but during an online exchange there's often no clear closure. It's also easy to continue after your Polite and Powerful statement; you may be tempted to try one more time to get your point across.

Why WAC Someone You Don't Know?

The fact that you don't know the other person at all is another reason that WAC'ing may not work. I see this in the Twitter wars that erupt between users who don't know each other personally but are following each other. Going back to the singer who bashed the reality star and the fan who tried to politely chastise the singer, the singer and the fan each tweeted about six or seven times, each one deepening instead of alleviating the conflict. I suppose that the fan came closest to a polite line when she initially wrote, and I'm translating from tweet speak here, "Always been a fan and defended you, but you shouldn't call 'her' out. Causes trouble."

The fan was right: the singer was causing trouble. But the singer made my point when she told her to "mind her own business." In fact, none of this was anyone's business. It may be simple to WAC someone via Twitter when you don't know the person. He or she can't fire you and you will probably never meet, but it can be hard to get a positive result. Even if you mean well, why bother? Life is stressful enough without jumping into the online drama and arguments of other people.

Move On

If the conflict is a minor issue or misunderstanding and you can simply text, message, post, or tweet a Polite and Powerful line: "I have a different opinion, so let's move on."

Then move on.

If someone apologizes to you, accept it. Then move on.

If you put something out there or posted a picture that someone did not like, own it and end it: "I'm sorry. I did not mean to insult you. I have taken it down." When you're the person who made the mistake, own it, apologize for it, and learn from it.

Then everybody needs to move on.

If it's really not a big deal and if the person really isn't that important in your life, then let it go.

Shut Down Heated Exchanges

But what if you can't move on?

Regardless of what you post or tweet, or who is responding to whom, if the conversation starts to get heated, you need to halt the exchange. Just stop. Social media is not the place to work out blossoming conflicts or disagreements. The key is to avoid a futile back-and-forth, especially with an aggressive person or with people you may not even know. It's simply not possible to fully express yourself in 140 characters or a comment box, not to mention the absence of helpful nonverbal communication.

Before any further engagement, I advise you to carefully consider who this person is in your life. If it's a high school acquaintance, chances are you will want to let it go. If it's a good friend who posted a picture of you in your bathing suit, well, that may be a different story! But if someone is just an annoying tweeter repeater or Facebook boaster, do you really care? Even if the Facebook boaster is a jerk, does it really hurt you? If you WAC him, is he going to change? Let the jerk speak for himself. You're probably not the only person who finds him annoying.

Take the Conversation Offline

Once you disengage from the heated exchange, you have a choice to make. Depending on who this person is in your life and how much you care about the relationship, you have three choices:

1. Do nothing right away. Take a day or two to think about what happened. Once you calm down, you may just let it go and continue with your life and your relationship.

2. Block or unfollow the person. If the person who offended you online is not a part of your offline world or is continuously annoying, just stop all online communication, and this means your online interest. Unlike people you have to deal with everyday, a lot of online people are easily avoided.

3. You can try to resolve the conflict offline. If you decide to have a discussion to resolve your differences, or if you want to WAC the person, the optimal scenario would be to meet in private but in a public place. (I don't suggest doing this with a stranger. It is *never* a good idea to meet alone with people offline whom you only know online.) Send a private message or email, letting the person know that you would like to meet: "We don't seem to be getting anywhere online. How about we meet for coffee and talk?" If a face-to-face-meeting is not possible, a phone call, for all of the reasons outlined in the last chapter, is the next best thing. If that can't happen, an email, following all of the guidelines for WAC'ing in writing, is your next best choice.

But What If Not Speaking Up Is Wrong?

What if something posted on social media goes beyond annoying? Emily told me about one of her Facebook "friends" who posted an image that was supposed to be humorous but was offensive. "I couldn't believe my eyes," she said. "I was just going to unfriend him and then I felt that I had an obligation to say something. People need to know when they're doing something wrong, or at least I need to tell the person my view." So she gave him a Polite and Powerful WAC: "Your post is not funny. It's racist and I am offended by it. Please stop."

More Tips for Avoiding Online Conflict

I hear a lot of stories from people who have learned their lessons on social media. Here is the wisdom they've shared with me.

1. Don't make negative comments about other people. If you have an issue with someone, address it. Why bother saying something that can make you, or the other person, look bad? Don't jump on the trash-the-celebrity bandwagon simply because you can. It's not Polite and Powerful behavior to make nasty comments about anyone, even public figures behaving badly. That person will likely never read what you've posted or tweeted, but you're showing others that you're capable of being nasty or judgmental. There is a way to comment on someone's behavior without attacking the person. There is a big difference between posting "X was an idiot for cheating," versus "It's sad to know that X hurt his spouse by cheating. Not a smart move."

2. Don't make negative commentary about your company or organization. Watercooler chat may be legal, but if you're saying something negative about your organization and it's online, there's written proof that you made those comments. In person, there's no permanent record. Even though it may not get you fired, saying negative things online won't get you promoted. Why bite the hand that feeds you? And as I mentioned earlier, if you are looking for work, your future employers will more than likely check your social media sites. Why would I hire someone who posts nasty things about past employers?

3. Keep your professional online activity separate from your personal. A journalism professor told me she was very surprised by professional journalists using Twitter to engage their audiences and then tweeting about how many drinks they had at the hotel bar or sending a Twitpic of themselves on vacation. If you use social media for professional reasons, you should also have separate business and personal accounts.

4. Don't get involved in other people's online arguments. If you feel you need to support one person over the other, do so privately. If you stick up for one friend over another, you may find yourself on the receiving end of a WAC.

5. Don't break up with someone online or via text—ever. This is just rude. One young woman texted her boyfriend of six years, "Our weekend plans are canceled. It's over between us." Ouch!

6. Respect people's privacy. Post photos and videos of others only with their permission. Even posting that you're having dinner with so-and-so may cause difficultly. One colleague had to WAC her friend and tell him not to post every time he had dinner with her. Other friends were hurt that they hadn't been invited, and she didn't want them to know.

7. Give yourself the jerk test. Consider how you use social media to share your views. If you are frequently tweeting or posting comments that inspire controversy or conflict, or if you've noticed that people have stopped responding to you, you may want to think about scaling back on your sharing. You may see yourself as just putting your opinion out there, but others may see it differently. In general, people don't like to be pontificated to or constantly told their opinion is incorrect. As already noted, many people have no idea they're being jerks. Let's face it, there are a lot of ways to be a jerk online without meaning to be.

Is It Time to Declutter Your Online Space?

In Part III of this book, we'll consider how to avoid conflict in your life, and evaluating your online activity and social media may be an important step. You know how every once in a while, you have to declutter your closet or garage because just opening the door causes your blood pressure to spike? Well, the same may be true for your online networks and "friendships." If you're feeling increasingly annoyed and aggravated by what others are posting and tweeting, maybe you need to declutter your online space too. Do you really need 786 Facebook friends? Do you really have to follow 4,000 people you don't know on Twitter?

More and more people are telling me that they're taking breaks from their online activity and smartphones. Unless your job demands it, why not take a timeout? An advertising executive told me she had finally "had it" with always being in touch on her smartphone and constantly checking Facebook and Twitter. Now when she comes home from work, she limits herself to an hour on the phone or computer. She then turns her phone off and spends time with her family (which leads to less conflict with her spouse).

People who reduce their online time report feeling better. They sleep better and experience less stress and conflict. In Part III, you'll find more ways to lower the stress and conflict in your life. Stay tuned!

14

Polite and Powerful for Other Difficult Situations

S o far you have learned the skills necessary to handle one type of difficult communication—the confrontation.

These same skills will empower you in new and surprising ways. Practice and adopt them, and your life will be less stressful and you'll feel better about yourself. A lot better.

But you're not out of the woods yet. There are more kinds of conversations and situations that fall into the category of "difficult communication" that you can handle Politely and Powerfully. Life is full of conversations or situations that make you nervous or uncomfortable. The kinds of conversations you'd love to avoid, but can't.

For instance, how do you tell someone:

You're quitting.
His fly is undone.
She's just been downsized.
His favorite uncle is in the hospital.

It's not easy delivering bad or embarrassing news. But there are times when you have to speak up in order to be fair to the other person. You shouldn't, for example, let a coworker walk around the rest of the day with broccoli in his teeth from lunch. This may sound silly, but it happens all the time.

On a more serious note, you have to have a conversation if you're planning on leaving your job. Though different from a confrontation, the kinds of difficult conversations we cover in this chapter have one important thing in common—how you handle yourself will have a significant impact on the outcome.

The skills you've learned thus far for Polite and Powerful confrontations, including the WAC'em model and your verbal and nonverbal skills, can be adapted and applied to more of life's difficult conversations and sticky situations. So too is the confidence you harness by handling yourself well. You'll feel empowered. You won't feel weighed down by dread when you have to tell somebody something she's probably not going to like hearing. You're less likely to speak harshly or use wimpy body language. You can neutralize difficult people simply by knowing how to handle yourself. It's so much easier going through life this way than the old way.

People have the same reaction in learning how to handle different types of difficult conversations as they do when they learn how to have Polite and Powerful confrontations. You have turned a corner. You never go back. You won't want to go back.

While a natural by-product of Polite and Powerful behavior in positive confrontations is a newfound freedom to "let it go," the opposite is true for other kinds of difficult conversations. You learn how to stop avoiding and dreading them. You can meet them head-on. You won't have to worry about them as much. You can be more direct. This is not to say that you'll always enjoy them. But when having the conversation is the right, or required, thing to do, you'll feel better about yourself knowing that you were direct and polite. You will then be in a better position to accept them as part of life.

When You Have a Choice and When You Don't

In some situations you will have to speak up. You have to tell Mark that his father is in the hospital. Clearly Mark needs to have this important information.

Sometimes you have a choice about whether or not to speak up. You believe your friend Caroline dresses inappropriately, while she thinks she dresses just fine. You think this could be why she's not getting promoted. Should you say something?

This is the kind of situation in which you have a choice. We'll get to the specifics of these conversations shortly.

What you always have a choice about is *how* you tell Mark and Caroline what you want or need to tell them. This is how everything you've learned in this book can help you. You now have a guide, a reservoir of skills, that you can use to handle just about any of life's difficult conversations with tact and honesty.

I have broken down the most difficult conversations into the three main areas that people typically dread, avoid, or feel embarrassed about:

1. Giving feedback
2. Giving bad news or unpleasant information
3. Expressing sympathy

1. Giving Feedback

"Sorry Sam, you're just not cutting it here in sales."
Telling someone he is not performing well or behaving appropriately is considered "feedback." So is telling someone something good, like she's getting a raise. But that's not hard. It's usually pleasant, so we're not going to deal with it in this chapter. What we are talking about here is feedback that may be difficult for another person to hear.

Sometimes you are required to give feedback. If you're a manager, school board president, or parent, it's part of your job. Sometimes you choose to give feedback because you believe it will help the person. There are four main feedback areas we'll discuss:

a. Not performing to a standard. This usually occurs in professional situations, but it can also occur with children.
b. Giving your unsolicited opinion.
c. Saving the person from further embarrassment.
d. Speaking up about unfair or unjust behavior.

How you give feedback to the other person in each of the above scenarios will depend on the situation. Let's look at each situation separately.

a. Not Performing to a Standard

If you're giving someone feedback about performing to an established or implied standard, you must first determine if you are the appropriate person. If you're the person's manager or the committee chairperson, then it is your job to give feedback. If you're the parent, it is your job to provide feedback to your child, such as, "Ben, please use your fork when you eat."

If you're not the appropriate person, giving feedback can be risky. And you know what happens to risk takers—they may be promoted, fired, or disliked.

When You Are the Appropriate Person, How Do You Proceed?

It's not easy to tell people things they don't want to hear.

But there are ways to do it that make it easier on both the other person and yourself. Back in the beginning of this book we considered one of the biggest components of positive confrontation: figuring out your words. What do you really want to say? The same is true for feedback conversations. This brings us back to Don't Attack'em, WAC'em.

Adapt Your WAC

WAC'em can easily be adapted as a model for giving people feedback. You can use it, or at least adapt it, to help you figure out what you want to say and possibly suggest how the person should be acting in the future.

Define the Problem Using Your W

What's wrong with the person's performance? Be specific. Don't expect anyone to understand what you mean by "lousy," "sloppy," or "not up to par." You must specifically explain what in the person's performance or behavior isn't working. Your W may be something like:

> Jason, you haven't attended the last three meetings.
> Your latest report had several spelling errors.

Every committee member is expected to work on one event a year. You haven't signed up for an event yet.

Your A: "Here's What I Need You to Do"

You're asking someone to change or modify his behavior to meet a standard. Following the above examples, your A would be something like:

Your attendance at all of our meetings is mandatory.

You need to use spell check regularly and find someone to proofread your documents.

We would like you to contribute too. Can you coordinate the bake sale?

Give the person a deadline for making improvements. In business, this may be dictated by company policy as well. The person may have thirty days to improve.

Your C: "Do I Have Your Agreement?"

As mentioned already, even if you have authority over the person, you still need to check in with her. The other person needs to have an opportunity to explain her behavior or to offer her thoughts. You may not be offering an option, but there may be extenuating circumstances in the person's life that you're simply not aware of. An employee may be caring for a sick parent or child or going through a personal crisis. You can be supportive and still be firm. If your company or organization offers resources such as counseling, encourage the person to take advantage of it.

"And If You Can't . . . "

Sometimes you need to explain what the consequences will be if the person cannot meet your expectations. Be clear. Be specific:

You won't be ready to get the promotion.

The monthly report will be assigned to someone else.

We'll have to ask you to resign your position on the committee.

Some other guidelines for giving your feedback:

- Do it in private. It's not appropriate to give people feedback in front of others. Six graduate students were having lunch with their professor. The professor remarked, "You have all become more confident in your lectures and that's great." But then he turned to Jackie and said, "Well, Jackie, you still have some problems with this." Not appropriate! While it was his job to give his students critical feedback, he should have made this kind of comment to Jackie in private.

- Balance the negative with the positive. If you can, find a way to note something positive: "You have errors in your report that detract from your terrific observations."

b. Giving Your Unsolicited Opinion

Here's another kind of feedback situation. And talk about sticky! Let's go back to the example of the friend who dresses inappropriately. You want to give her feedback. You haven't been asked to do so and you're not required to do it. However, you think it might help her get promoted.

Be careful, this is touchy stuff.

The other person may not be receptive to feedback. After all, she hasn't asked you for it. Before you say a word, you need to ask yourself, "Why am I doing this? Am I really concerned about this person? Am I really just putting her down?" You must consider the person; will she be open to your comments? You may harm your relationship.

A friend had a mole on her face. It was unattractive and perhaps unhealthy. I risked it and told her that I once had a mole removed for health reasons. That opened the door for me to suggest she get hers looked at. She did and had it removed.

Sometimes people use personal bias as a reason to WAC someone. Julia wanted to WAC a good friend for posting "stupid quotes" on his Facebook wall several times a week.

When I asked why the comments bothered her, she shrugged and said, "I don't want to block him and it's annoying. He does it all the time." I asked her if the quotes were offensive in any way. "No," she said. "They're the inspirational ones." When I asked if he was doing any harm, she had to admit that he wasn't. In this case, it wasn't her place to WAC a person whose Facebook posts simply annoyed her. I advised her that if she thought this would be good feedback for him to hear, that she have to a face-to-face conversation instead of telling him via Facebook.

A woman told me about a friend with an unattractive hairstyle. Other than this one blip, her appearance was attractive. Should she tell her?

If she chooses to say something, she has the following options.

- She can be direct: "I like your hair better the other way," if she believed her friend was open to hearing comments like that.

- She can be indirect. "What made you decide to change your hair?" This question would get the conversation going.

- She can wait until asked for her opinion and then be honest— but Politely and Powerfully: "Now that you ask, I liked your hair better the other way."

Ellen's friend Matthew wore thick glasses. She thought he'd look better in contact lenses. But when she told him her opinion, he told her, "My eye doctor told me I can't wear contacts. Do you really think I look that bad?" Oops.

"Donated" opinions cause a lot of conflict in families, where people freely offer one another criticisms. Three sisters finally had to put a moratorium on this behavior because they realized they were constantly fighting over comments like, "Your new hair color makes your complexion look pale."

My sisters and I are more direct. I once got in the car and one of them turned to me and said, "Phew, you stink." I had too much perfume on. I laughed. This is just how we are and it works for us.

You will have to evaluate whether or not to engage conversations on a case-by-case basis. But follow two important guidelines. First, express concern for the person. You can say, "I care about you doing well" or "I thought you would want to know this."

Second, if the person isn't receptive to your comments, drop it. Don't react in a way that is insulting to the other person. You wouldn't say, "I thought you could handle the truth" or "I forgot how sensitive you are."

Then let it go.

But what if the other person asks for your opinion? Give it, but remember that this isn't a license to forget polite behavior. So you wouldn't say to a friend, "I'm so glad you asked me that because I've been dying to tell you that you dress too provocatively." You're going to make her feel worse.

Better wording would be, "Women managers dress pretty conservatively here. I would lower my skirts and not show any cleavage."

c. Saving the Person from Further Embarrassment

"Psst . . . I thought I should tell you, your barn door is open!"

When you don't live on a farm, what does this mean?

A physician who was told this in front of a group of interns didn't know either. He kept asking, "What's a barn door?" He discovered later that his fly was undone.

Here is the first rule for giving someone feedback in an embarrassing situation: be direct. Don't use innuendo, code words, or hand signals to deliver your message. If the person's fly is undone, simply describe the situation: "Tom, your fly is undone."

Sometimes that's all it takes. But keep these points in mind:

- Do speak up. Generally, it's better to let the person know he has a big piece of spinach on his front tooth or the dreaded toilet paper tail on her heel. You will be saving the person further embarrassment.

When my friend was in law school, a professor walked into the auditorium to lecture from the stage. He had his fly undone. I asked if anybody said anything. He said no.

I was horrified. "You let him lecture that way for two hours?"

"Yep. We didn't like him."

• Be discreet. Don't shout or tell the person so others can hear. A Polite and Powerful person would never embarrass another person this way. Making a joke out of another person's situation is mean-spirited. You always want to be discreet. A motivational speaker was giving a great talk to his audience, walking from person to person, interacting with them, but his fly was undone. No one said anything for ten minutes. A woman he passed by gave him a note that told him. He didn't blink an eye and fixed the fly without missing a beat.

If the person responds negatively, be Polite and Powerful anyway. If you tell someone his fly is down and he says, "What are you looking down there for?" don't go there. Simply say, "I'm surprised by your response. I thought you would have wanted to know."

• Simply describe the situation. "Your bra strap is showing." This is really the W, and nothing else needs to be said. Also, don't touch without permission. If a woman has her back zipper undone, don't just fix it for her without asking permission to do so. A woman once went to remove a hair from another woman's chin and it was attached! There's another awful oops.

• Send an emissary. If you're embarrassed because of gender, ask someone else to do it. My husband and I were at a party. A woman's bra strap was showing. Marty said to me, "Why don't you go tell her?" He asked me because he thought it would be less embarrassing for the woman. I did it. The woman was grateful.

- Drop the subject quickly. Don't dwell on whatever it was. Just let it go.

d. Speaking Up About "Unfair" or "Unjust" Behavior

Earlier in the book, I advised you to let something go if it's not your issue. The way to determine what is or isn't your issue is by gauging the effect another person's behavior has on you. If it doesn't have a direct effect, then it's not really your issue and you wouldn't WAC the person about that issue.

But what happens when you repeatedly see your coworker arriving late and leaving early when the boss is out of the office? If he is asking you to cover for him and you feel uncomfortable doing so, you have a pretty clear WAC'em: "I don't feel comfortable covering for you so you can leave early" (your W). "Please don't ask me to do this anymore, okay?" (your A and C).

But suppose he doesn't ask you to cover for him. Suppose his comings and goings do not affect your workload directly, but his actions, and the fact that he's getting away with it, may bother you. Should you speak up and give him this feedback?

Here's another scenario. Suppose there's a handicap parking space in your condo development. You have a neighbor who ignores the sign and parks there anyway. You're not entitled to park in this spot either, so it's not like she's taking your spot. But her behavior is driving you crazy. You believe she has no right to park there.

In both of these scenarios, the effect on you is not direct—you don't have more work and you still have your parking spot—but you still feel affected. You perceive the person's behavior as unfair or unjust. You're annoyed. What can you do about it? Should you speak up?

Before you speak up, make sure:

- You have *all* of the information. Don't label the person a jerk until you know for sure that your coworker hasn't received permission to leave early. Maybe he's working at home or has a sick relative. Maybe the woman parking in the spot has recently had an operation. If you don't have all the facts, you can't assess whether or not it's worth it to say something.

- It is really worth it. I understand that you may feel outrage when you see another person do something that you think is unfair. But I also know that if you frequently let yourself be affected by what you perceive as unjust behavior, you are going to spend a good deal of your time feeling indignant and outraged. This is not a positive, energizing way to go through life. I have also found that people who grumble about "injustice" may sometimes be transferring their frustrations about one thing into another. Watch out for this behavior too; it's draining.

- Approach the person in a respectful manner. Talk to the person and ask for clarification. Make sure you keep it simple: "Are you aware that this is handicap parking?" or "How come you park in the handicap spot?" You can also describe the behavior or the perceived injustice: "I've noticed that when the boss isn't here you come in late and leave early." You may learn something you didn't know or your comment may be all it takes for the person to stop parking in the spot or leaving early. But watch your non-verbal signals, especially your tone of voice. Keep it neutral. You don't want to pick a fight.

- Use common sense. If you are concerned about the person's reaction, I wouldn't approach the person directly.

- Decide whether you want to go over the person's head. You can go to your manager and say, "I believe it's important for you to know that Connor comes in late and leaves early when you're not here."

Even if you follow all of these guidelines, I still can't tell you to go out and do this. Each person must make up his or her mind according to the situation and people involved. I do suggest that you consider the repercussions to your own professional image, office, and other relationships. Will you be perceived as a tattletale? A busybody? A hero? Will your coworker find out that you said something and then hold it against you?

However, in the case of the handicap parking violator, you can report this person to your condo association or your security personnel at work and let them handle it. In some cases, you could even call the police and report it. But I think you should call the police as a last resort. It's usually best to approach people directly when and if possible.

2. Giving Bad News or Unpleasant Information

"I hate to have to be the one to tell you this, but . . . "

The second main area of difficult conversation deals with giving bad news. You have to tell someone something you know she does not want to hear. No wonder we try to get out of having these conversations. Is there a nice way to say, "You didn't get the job" or "You know how we promised you that shipment would be on time, well . . . " or "I know you've been looking forward to this trip for weeks but . . . "

David Letterman used to have a segment on his show where he would call someone and break some news on behalf of an audience member who couldn't bring himself or herself to do it. It was often funny, yet I couldn't help wondering what would be the consequences to both parties later. After all, the person on the receiving end was ambushed on national television.

While I think it's a terrible idea to deliver news like this, it does illustrate a great point—people will go to great lengths to get out of having an unpleasant conversation. They don't know what to say or how to say it. But in doing this, they usually make things worse. If you don't tell the person, someone else may. Then you have to deal with, "Why didn't *you* tell me?"

Every summer for five years in a row, Karen and Don vacationed at the beach with their close friends, Vicky and Jim. Karen and Don were ready for a change of scenery and wanted to vacation alone. It wasn't that the couple didn't like their friends anymore; they just wanted to make this change.

Karen agonized about how to tell Vicky. She was afraid of hurting her feelings. She agonized so much that finally Don couldn't stand it anymore.

The next time the two couples were together he said, "I think you know how much we love hanging out with you guys. The thing is, we've made a decision to take a different vacation this summer. We want to go away alone."

As it turned out, Vicky and Jim were thinking of doing something different too. Karen could have saved herself a lot of trouble by being up front sooner.

By using the skills you've learned in this book, you'll be able to make this kind of conversation easier on the other person and yourself. Keep these points in mind when you're facing one of those "breaking it gently" conversations:

a. Have a face-to-face conversation, if possible. You now know why this it is usually better than an email or a phone call.

b. Talk in private. You don't announce in a meeting that one of your team members did not win the employee of the year award. You need to let him know first.

c. Avoid starting with something ominous like, "I don't know how to tell you this, but . . . " You do know, and you're doing it. It's better to be direct and say, "I have some bad news" or "There's been a change of plans" and then just say what you have to say.

d. Explain but don't go overboard. Offer the reasons, if appropriate. Explain but maintain your Polite and Powerful behavior and language. Don't make excuses or apologize: "We want to take a private vacation because, well, we're having some marital problems." Too much information! Keep it simple. "We want to go away by ourselves this year." If you have to tell someone she didn't get the promotion or the raise, you need to tell her why, even though it may be tough for her to hear. A woman was told that she didn't get the promotion to sales manager because she was too soft spoken and seemed passive. She appreciated knowing and was able to work on her nonverbal behavior.

e. Offer to help or give the person alternatives, if possible. A woman I know had been dreaming of visiting her mother's birthplace in Italy. Her husband had promised to take her on their tenth wedding anniversary, but when the time came, he was having some financial problems. While he dreaded telling his wife, he did something smart to help soften the bad news. He pulled out an account book and said, "I've just opened this vacation account. I am going to put twenty-five dollars a week into it and extra when I can. In a couple of years, we'll have the money."

"Your uncle is in the hospital."

In this situation, it's best to be direct and say, "I'm so sorry. Your Uncle Vince is in the hospital." Don't be dramatic and don't delay by saying, "I'd like you to sit down before I tell you this" or "I know you're going to be very upset when you hear this." You should never keep people in suspense. It is usually clear from your body language and tone of voice that something is terribly wrong, so just tell the person what has happened.

Soften Bad News with Positive News When You Can

If you can, start with the better news first. When Beth's husband had a serious car accident, she appreciated the way her sister told her what had happened. "Beth," she said, "everything is okay now. Gary is going to be fine, except he was in a car accident."

If she had said, "Gary has been in a terrible car accident," Beth said she would have fainted on the spot. I probably would too.

"I quit."

You're moving on to another job or company, or you're making a lifestyle change that doesn't include full-time employment. This isn't bad news for you but can be difficult news to give to your boss.

Laurie had been working for three years as the marketing director of a publishing company. She had a long commute—two hours each way—and she wanted to start working part-time and closer to home. This normally self-assured woman was a walking nerve ending about telling her boss. She had no idea what she was going to say.

"Can't you just tell him that you've decided to leave the company?" I suggested.

"Yes," she said. "But I feel bad."

"Why?" I asked. "Did you sign a contract or break a promise?"

"No."

"Did you work hard for three years?"

"Of course."

"You're not bound to this job," I told her, "or obligated to your boss for life."

"I didn't think of it that way," she said.

This seems to be a common problem. We feel obligated or afraid of the other person's reaction. As long as you're not obligated by contract to stay and as long as you're giving proper notice, simply tell your boss, Politely and Powerfully, that you're leaving.

Laurie was full of ideas about what she would say. I suggested, "Pretend I'm your boss. Practice on me."

It was a good thing we did this because the first thing out of her mouth was a nervous laugh. Her body language also conveyed nervousness. Then she said, "Gee, I feel so bad about this, but I have to tell you how sorry I am but I need to quit."

Talk about self-discounting language and behavior! I stopped her right there and gave her these guidelines:

a. **Plan what you're going to say.** Write the words down.

b. **Practice.** You're going to be nervous. Get a friend to role-play with you.

c. **Don't apologize.** If you haven't done anything wrong, don't say you're sorry for leaving.

You can say, "I'm sad to be leaving this great group of people. I'll miss everyone, but it's time for me to move on." Don't say, "I'm sorry, you're going to hate me, I know you're really busy and this is the last thing you need." And don't apologize with your nonverbals. If you knot yourself up in your chair, wring your hands, or play with your hair, you're not going to look like a person who has just made an important decision.

d. **Keep it simple.** Here is simple: "I have another opportunity that I've decided to take."

Don't give someone your life story and make excuses. You're not obligated to fill your boss in on all the details. How much you choose to share

204 • THE POWER OF POSITIVE CONFRONTATION

will depend on your relationship. But for your initial conversation, keep it short and simple.

e. Prepare a Polite and Powerful line. If you think the person may try to argue with you or try to talk you out of your decision, go in with a line prepared to expresses your Polite and Powerful position, like, "I appreciate your concern, but I've made my decision." No matter what argument the person may pose, just keep repeating your line. "I understand that you want me to stay and I'm grateful for the counteroffer, but I've made my decision." Stick to your line, unless, of course, you are made an offer you can't refuse.

f. Don't burn your bridges. If you've had elaborate fantasies about "telling your boss off" or cluing him in to how lazy your coworkers really are—forget it. I've heard story after story of bridge burners who lived to regret their actions. Telling someone off doesn't make you feel better for more than ten adrenaline-packed minutes. Then you feel lousy. Nothing changes except now you've lost a reference. Jeff learned this the hard way: "I was looking forward to quitting my job. I had gotten to the point where I hated my boss. He was a terrible manager and didn't treat everyone fairly. I told him off pretty good. I could tell he was pretty shocked. He said 'I always thought we had a good relationship. Why didn't you speak up sooner?' He seemed so sincere. I felt like a jerk."

I read a news story about a woman who gleefully photographed herself quitting her job with a series of dry erase board messages, which included a lot of details about how she hated her boss and that his breath smelled bad, that she emailed to her entire company. Yes, it was a creative way to quit, but now in her industry, she'll always be known as the woman who quit by sending out 33 pictures of herself saying vengeful things about her former boss.

Don't make negative comments about your former boss, coworkers, or organization, and not on social media either. You never know who might read it (even a potential employer) and hold it against you. I also heard a story about a man who left his company and then posted to a website where people vent about companies and organizations. Though it's anonymous, the person posted information that was so specific it was obvious to his former employer exactly who he was. The man received a letter from the company's attorney threatening a libel suit.

3. Expressing Sympathy

"I'm sorry for your loss, but trust me, it's better this way."

Our third and last area of difficult conversation is one we all have to deal with sooner or later: expressing our condolences when someone's loved one has died. Yes, this is hard. It's natural to feel awkward and tongue-tied in this kind of situation. Yet it is a mistake to avoid saying something to a grieving person. It's understandable that people feel awkward and don't want to upset the person. I often hear, "I worry that I'll make him feel worse."

You probably won't. *It's important to say something.* It is incredibly helpful for the person who has experienced the loss of a loved one to hear expressions of sympathy from others. Often people come to understand this when they themselves are in the throes of loss. They realize how much they appreciate hearing from people who also knew the deceased and are also saddened by the loss.

So what exactly do you say? It isn't your job to try to cheer up the person or convince him he can handle it. Your job is simply to offer support. A good rule of thumb is not to offer assurances ("Time heals all wounds" or "Your father is in a better place") or directives ("Be grateful for the time you had" or "She would want you to be happy"). Comforting words can be as simple as:

> I'm so sorry for your loss.
> I know this must be a difficult time for you and your family.
> You're in my thoughts.

People often say, "I know what you're going through," and maybe you think you do, but the grieving person may be too overwhelmed to know what she is feeling or experiencing, so how can you? Saying "I can't imagine what you're going through" acknowledges the enormity of the loss.

It's also okay to let the person know what you will miss about the person, or what you will remember. "Your mom always had a big smile, and I will miss hearing her laugh."

Don't make predictions about when the person will feel better, but if you can, share some of your own experience. "I lost my dad last year. The holidays were rough, but it does get easier."

If you use a commercial sympathy card, that's fine, but add a handwritten note to it. Simply signing your name is too impersonal. People who are grieving want to hear from their loved ones and friends, not the greeting card company's writer:

> She was a wonderful person and I know how much she will be missed.
> Your father often talked about you. He told me often that you were a special person to him. He was so proud of you.

If you add personal information about the person, the grieving family can read the note again and again for comfort.

The Benefit of Having Difficult Conversations

As you can see, instead of avoiding or dreading difficult conversations, you can put your WAC'em words and verbal and nonverbal skills to work in helping you have other kinds of difficult conversations. Whether you need to put an employee on a performance improvement plan or tell your close friends you don't want to vacation with them this year, knowing how to conduct all types of difficult conversations is empowering. Time you used to spend dreading, avoiding, or worrying is now free time you can use in a creative or constructive way.

15

When You Get WAC'ed

B y now, you should have a pretty clear idea of what it takes to handle
yourself Politely and Powerfully during a confrontation or a difficult
conversation. You now understand how to handle the other person—
no matter how he or she reacts.

But what happens if you're the one getting WAC'ed?

Believe me, it's bound to happen—even Polite and Powerful people
make mistakes and do bothersome things by accident. You are probably
going to do something that someone else finds annoying, unacceptable,
and possibly even offensive. Maybe you'll have no idea. Maybe you'll be
surprised. "What? Me?"

You may get WAC'ed by someone or someone may give you feedback,
either about job performance or something personal. You may be the person whose blouse is unbuttoned or whose fly is open.

Relax. We all need feedback to grow. Constructive criticism or honest
feedback can be helpful. Have you ever met someone who can't handle
criticism? Usually these people are annoying because you can't tell them
anything.

I personally would rather know if I was doing something to annoy another person than not know. If a client suddenly drops me, you bet I want
to learn why. It may be because their training needs or budget has changed,
but if it's something I have done to lose the business, it's critical that I
find out. I especially want to know if my blouse has accidentally come
unbuttoned!

What You Need to Know If You Get WAC'ed

Everyone in the world makes mistakes.

You're not perfect. Start getting over that now if it is a problem for you.

If Your Fly Is Down, Pull It Up And Keep On Smiling

Who doesn't look foolish now and then? Even Polite and Powerful people will drag the banner of toilet paper behind them, have spinach leaves stuck in their teeth, trip over their own feet, and have other embarrassing things happen to them.

It's not what happens to you that matters. It's how you handle what happens to you that matters.

During a big seminar I was giving I was wearing a cordless mike. At the first break, I forgot about it and went to the ladies room—with the mike on! One of the women ran in and told me, but not until it was too late.

I had to go back in. But how do you go back into a room with sixty people who have just heard you relieving yourself in the bathroom? You just do it. I had only one real choice—I had to laugh at myself. I went back in, and with a totally serious expression on my face, I said, "There's a theory which states that you have to have a significant emotional experience in order to change your behavior." I paused and then said, "Well, ladies and gentleman, I just had quite a significant emotional experience. I will never, as long as I live, forget to turn off my microphone!"

The entire roomful of people broke out laughing.

Of course I was embarrassed, but since I handled it with humor and grace, this situation helped build rapport with my audience. It would have been worse to pretend it never happened.

You Need Feedback to Improve

We get job reviews to find out how we're doing. Even though we may not want to hear about something we're doing wrong, wouldn't you rather hear it so you can fix it?

These are general guidelines for handling yourself when you are on the receiving end of criticism, feedback, or a WAC:

1. Don't get defensive. Going on the defensive when you meet with critical feedback or when you get WAC'ed is the least constructive thing you can do. I know this can be hard, but keep an open mind. Hear your critics, listen to the comments. Accept that you may at times offend someone. If you don't "hear" and "accept" you let others have power over you. You twist in the wind of resentment, insecurity, and defensiveness. This is no way to live.

After every seminar, I give my participants feedback cards. Occasionally I'll get a negative comment. I used to think, "Oh no, they hate me. Maybe the whole seminar was a bomb." But that wouldn't be the case at all. Over time, I have learned not to hit the panic button, but to think about feedback and learn from it. I have learned to consider the bad and the good. I always carefully consider the feedback I get. After all, if it can help make my future seminars better, I'm all for it.

Megan is a sports blogger on a popular website. Being one of the few women bloggers in the still male-dominated field of sports, she has had her sports knowledge questioned just because she is a woman, but sometimes not. "Eventually I had to realize that not all comments were driven by sexist motives," she said. "Sometimes these critics have a point and I can actually learn from them. They keep me on my toes. A few of them have become regular readers who will also leave positive comments when they feel I've made a good point or written an especially good blog."

2. Consider the source. If I have fifty comment cards or blog comments that say "you're great" and one that says "you were boring," what am I supposed to think? If the one person doesn't give me a reason, I dismiss the comment. For all I know, maybe I look like his ex-wife or her ex-best friend. If the comment is specific, however, regarding the content of a seminar or my delivery, then I consider the feedback carefully.

I ask myself, "Who is the person giving me the feedback? Is he or she an expert or a jerk? Does the person know what he or she is talking about?" If the person is an expert, the feedback is a gift. And you are fortunate to get that kind of advice from that caliber of person. If an expert gives me feedback, I seriously weigh what that person had told me.

My speech coach, the one who told me she knew I was from the East Coast by the mistakes I made in my speech, provided feedback that was important for me to hear. Without it, I would have kept right on making those mistakes in my presentations. It may be a small thing, but the small things can bring your image and reputation down too.

And so what if the person is a jerk? If the person is a jerk and I mean a true jerk, be polite, thank the person, and put the feedback on the back burner in your mind.

3. Is this an isolated incident? One random comment here or there usually means a lot more about the person who is giving you the comment than its validity. Once I received the following comment: "Barbara, you should never wear wedge heels. They make your ankles look thick." In all the 2,100 seminars I have given, I only received that one once! Chances are that comment had a lot more to do with that person's perception of women in heels rather than my ankle size.

Yet if you start getting feedback from a number of people and/or situations that are very similar, chances are there is some validity to the comments and you should consider them carefully. If three people you know and respect tell you, "You talk too fast," you better sit back and consider that it may be true.

4. Consider how the other person handles the conversation/confrontation. Chances are, you might not simply get WAC'ed, but you may get WAC'ed by someone who doesn't have the same skills that you now do. In other words, you will be at the mercy of whatever confrontational skills and style the other person has (or doesn't have). But you're not helpless. Knowing the skills you've learned in this book, there are lots of ways you can save the situation and handle yourself politely and powerfully. Here is what to do if:

- The person is aggressive. You don't expect someone to calmly discuss an issue with you if you're shouting at her or shaking your fist at him. The same goes in reverse. Someone may have the right to WAC you, but she doesn't have the right to be aggressive or rude. If this happens, you can say, "I very much want to hear your thoughts, but I can't listen to you if you're yelling at me."

- The person is passive. If the person is apologizing profusely, tell her there is no need to be sorry: "You just need to tell me what's going on."

- The person is not clear on the W and A. If you feel the person is being vague or not specific about his W and you're not clear on what you're doing that is bothering him, ask for clarification. You need to know the person's W and A. Before you learned WAC'em, you may have had a hard time clarifying your thoughts and understanding what was bothering you and what you wanted in its place. The other person may be having this difficulty too. Rephrase what he is saying and repeat it back to him: "Let me be clear. You're saying that when I made that comment about your girlfriend, you thought I was saying she was a jerk?" Or "I understand that you want me to stop leaving my laundry in the washing machine."

Your Response

You will usually have to respond to the person, whether or not you agree with what, or how, she has told you. Here are some guidelines to help you handle your response:

1. If you're wrong, apologize. You love it when you WAC the other person and she realizes you're right. So again, in reverse, you need to be the person who recognizes a mistake. "You're right," can go a long way to resolving conflict and mending wounded relationships. But don't over-apologize or make excuses. If you've made a mistake, one hearty and sincere "I'm sorry about that" is enough. Don't make excuses for your behavior if you're wrong. "Well, you see, I haven't been sleeping well and my brother is in the hospital and the holidays are coming up." You're going to sound like a jerk if you make excuses.

I remember reading about a journalist who had been caught taking too much creative license by fabricating an interview. He gave a statement in the publication that was full of excuses: "A loved one is sick and I've been under pressure." I read that and I thought, "I would have had respect for you if you had just said, 'I made a mistake. I was wrong.'"

2. Why not give the person his or her A? If what the person is asking for is no big deal, or you really don't mind, then why not do it? If it makes your spouse crazy that you leave dishes in the sink, why not put them in the dishwasher? Even simple gestures can go a long way to keeping relationships healthy and happy.

3. If you disagree, discuss the issue. If you really don't like the person's A, then suggest another alternative. Explain how you feel or what you think is a workable compromise.

4. You can ask the person to handle it differently in the future. If the person didn't WAC you in an appropriate way, ask her to change this behavior in the future. "From now on, if you have a problem with me, please come to me right away. I'd rather clear it up right away, than let it get to this point. Okay?"

5. If the person has power over you, you may not be able to discuss the issue. If the person is your manager or supervisor, you may have no choice but to agree. I'm not talking about ethical issues, such as someone asking you to do something you don't think is right or legal, just the practical ones. If your manager wants the report formatted a certain way, even if you think it looks better another way, she's the boss. You may have to do it her way.

6. Maintain positive nonverbal behavior. Try to keep your arms open. It's a natural defense mechanism to cross our arms when we feel threatened. But you're not under threat, so unfold them. Open body language shows that you are open to hearing the other person's thoughts. It will make you look Polite and Powerful. Try to tune in to your facial expression too. Don't scowl. Try to keep a neutral expression on your face.

7. Listen. One of the most important things you can do when you get WAC'ed is to listen. When you WAC others, you want them to listen to you and take you seriously. It's only right that you do the same in return. Review the box in Chapter 9 for reminders on how to be a good listener.

8. If you get upset, try to pull yourself together. You may be caught off guard and you may get emotional. It happens. If you feel like you might cry or you're getting very upset and are afraid of blowing your lid, ask to leave for a moment or two. Go somewhere quiet and pull yourself together. Tell yourself you can handle it Politely and Powerfully, and then go back and finish the discussion. If you're still too upset, reschedule for another time.

WAC'em Helps You Receive Criticism

People tell me they love WAC'em because it helps them both give feedback to others and receive it themselves. Try to keep an open mind if you receive feedback or get WAC'ed. Don't be afraid to see your own rough spots. We all have them; it's how we deal with them that counts. People who get defensive, the ones you can't say anything to, are often annoying to others.

Conclusion to Part II

You've come a long way and you've assimilated a lot of important information. Let's take a breath and recap for a moment. In Part II of this book you learned how to:

- WAC instead of attack. You now have a fast and effective way for gathering your words for a confrontation or difficult conversation. You know how to specifically define what's bothering you. And what you want the other person to do. You can use your WAC'em card until you can get your words together easily on your own.

- How to interact with the other person during a confrontation. You check in with the other person to see if what you've asked for is possible. You should have a discussion if you disagree. Try to work out a mutually acceptable alternative. You know what to do if the other person is not Polite and Powerful—you stay Polite and Powerful no matter how tempted you are to do otherwise.

- Use your verbal and nonverbal skills to help you have a positive confrontation. You know that self-discounting language, negative words, and bad diction are some of the verbal vices that can lessen the positive impact of your WAC. On the nonverbal side, good control over your body language, tone of voice, facial expression, and eye contact is important to your success as well.

- Choose how to WAC the person. WAC'ing someone in person, in writing, or over the phone are all options. While it's usually best to WAC someone in person, you can also do it in writing and over the phone.

- Handle yourself Politely and Powerfully during other kinds of difficult conversations—giving feedback, including unsolicited advice, giving bad or unpleasant news, and expressing sympathy. Don't try to avoid having these conversations and don't worry about them either. Adapt your WAC and employ the verbal and nonverbal skills you've learned.

PART III

Conflict-Free Living

16

The Secret to Avoiding Conflict in Life

n Part II of this book, you learned many useful tools to help you handle conflict successfully. You will soon, if you haven't already, discover how much better you will feel when you know that you can approach any difficult situation or difficult conversation with poise and confidence. When it comes to conflict, there's only one thing better—not to be in the difficult situation or need to have the difficult conversation in the first place.

Of course, no one can have zero conflict in life. You'd be living under a rug or inside a very big bubble if you had a totally conflict-free life. But you can move toward having less conflict in your day-to-day life, whether in person or online. I've seen many people do it. You can do it too. Actually, you've already started moving toward zero. You took your first step to a more positive way of life when you learned (and continue to practice) WAC'ing people instead of attacking them.

Another step you took is learning (and practicing) effective verbal and nonverbal communication.

Yet another is learning how to handle difficult conversations.

You're pretty close. But you can get even closer by learning to avoid *causing* conflict and learning how to be the kind of person who treats others with respect, kindness, and understanding. If you use these positive behaviors, you will be able to establish rapport and make a connection with others.

Like so many changes I prescribe in this book for less stressful living, learning how to establish rapport is pretty simple. Yet make no mistake;

the positive effect on your life can be profound. When you are able to connect with others in a positive way, you feel good about the people around you *and* you feel good about yourself. In turn, others will feel good about interacting with you.

What "Rapport" Means for You

So what exactly, in the context of this discussion, does "establishing rapport" mean? The *American Heritage Dictionary* defines the word "rapport" as: "A relationship, esp. one of mutual trust or emotional affinity." Sounds good. For our purposes though, we need a little more information. I therefore add the following: "achieved, in part, through common courtesy and practicing good etiquette."

I'd also like to make the distinction between minor and major rapport. Saying hello to the clerk who checks out your groceries is an example of minor rapport. You may not want to establish a long-term relationship with him, but why not be friendly? It will usually make your checkout interaction more pleasant.

An example of major rapport would be having a conversation with, and getting to know, a neighbor or someone you meet at a trade show or convention. This is a person with whom you may want to have an ongoing relationship or add to your LinkedIn network.

Keep in mind that establishing *both* major and minor rapport with others is important. Both will impact the quality of your life and reduce the amount of conflict in your life. When you are friendly to clerks in grocery stores and friendly with your neighbors, it's much more likely that these people, in turn, will be friendly to you.

Beyond Minding Your Manners

Because good rapport requires good etiquette skills, this chapter is mostly about etiquette, but in a specific context. Yes, minding your manners involves saying "please," "thank-you," and "have a nice day." That's not new.

What is new is learning and using Polite and Powerful language and many other etiquette skill areas to:

- Handle yourself with grace, poise, and good humor in a world where these things often seem rare.

- Get along with your coworkers, neighbors, and new people you happen to meet.

- Get along with people you don't know.

- Establish better rapport with the people you already have professional or personal relationships with.

The Benefits of Good Rapport

Knowing how to establish and build rapport with others will help you avoid conflict in many areas of your life. Reduced conflict is the main benefit you'll experience. There are others:

You'll meet other people more easily. You'll feel confident in what can sometimes be awkward situations. You can make small talk with anyone. People will welcome your presence.

I know it sounds almost too simple to be true. How can good rapport achieved through good etiquette skills bring all of these terrific things to your life? But it is true. Etiquette skills can be invaluable. So many of us just don't know the rules of modern etiquette. And to make things even more complicated, many of us don't know that some of the rules have changed. This lack of knowledge causes problems, arguments, misunderstandings, and sometimes even serious conflicts.

I'm going to talk about the etiquette areas essential to establishing and maintaining good rapport. If you learn these skills, your life will be generally less full of conflict than it currently may be. You'll even have days when your conflict thermometer hovers at zero.

The reason is simple. You get back what you put in. People respond to how you treat them. A key point to remember is that it's hard to be nasty to people who are nice to you.

Twelve Simple Ways to Establish Rapport

To brush up on your rapport-building skills there are twelve life-enhancing, relationship-building skills that you'll need to learn and practice. The twelve I describe here may seem like little things, and each one taken on its own can be. But taken as a whole, they can make a huge difference in how we connect, or fail to connect, with others. The best part is, they're easy to learn and simple to use. You can read this chapter, put this book down, go out into the world, and start.

All you have to do is remember them and put them into practice.

1. Greet and Acknowledge Others

This first skill is the most simple and most powerful: greet and acknowledge people. Say hello, good morning, how are you? good-bye.

Many people are astonished that this is number 1 on my list. To the doubters, a hello or good morning seems too simple or trivial, but it is number 1 for a reason. Failing to say hello or good-bye is a big source of conflict. People don't like to be ignored.

Claudia told me how she was having a drink with some colleagues after work. One of the women, who was fairly new to the organization, went to the ladies room and then left the bar without saying good-bye. Claudia thought this was very rude, and she later discovered that her co-workers wondered if the woman was antisocial.

When you see people you know or even those you don't know, you should look them in the eye and say something—hello, good morning, how are you. This establishes a human connection between you and the other person. It's as if you are saying, "I see you. You have become part of my day. You are on my radar screen."

You certainly don't have to walk around all day parroting hello over and over again, but when you cross paths with someone, you should acknowledge the person.

How Do You Feel About People Who Don't Say Hello to You?

Recently I had a stress test. The doctor had me talking during the test. He asked what I do for living. I said I teach etiquette and assertiveness in corporations and organizations. He said, "Please teach my technician that when I say good morning to him, he needs to respond back. It drives me crazy that he doesn't!"

People really dislike it when others fail to greet them, and it happens all the time.

You probably don't like people who don't greet you. In fact, you are probably pretty quick to make a negative assumption about them as rude, unfriendly, or self-important. Then it becomes tempting to withhold being nice in return.

I'm truly amazed sometimes that I need to tell people to say hello to others. Here is how I put it: "If someone says hello to you, you *have* to say hello back. It is not optional."

Of course I'm not talking about meeting someone in a dark alley; in that case, you don't even say good-bye, you just run. The rest of the time, when you're safe and comfortable, say hello.

Look Up!

You usually make eye contact when you greet someone. Yet in today's world of texting while walking, people are looking at their phones and consequently avoid greeting others. The person that you say hello to on the way to the interview or sales meeting may in fact be the person who will be interviewing you or potentially buying your product. Establishing minor rapport in this way will help you have a successful meeting.

A communications professor once told me that when she walks down the busy and narrow hallways at her college, she routinely has to tell students to look up because they are paying attention to their screens and are practically colliding with her.

The Impact of a Greeting

The whole atmosphere of any organization, be it a major corporation or a book group, can be changed when people say good morning, have a nice day, or how are you.

You do not need to know someone to offer a simple, pleasant good morning. As I mentioned earlier, minor rapport is always important to establish. If you move into a new neighborhood and you see a new neighbor across the street, what do you do? Do you say hello or wave? There are people who tell me they don't greet their neighbors because they don't want to get too involved.

Saying hello isn't getting involved; it's simply being polite. Acknowledging a person doesn't mean inviting him to dinner (though you certainly can do so). It just means you are aware of others around you and are a pleasant person. How can this be bad?

Don't tell me this doesn't work; it evens affects major league baseball players. In an ESPN story, Carl Crawford said, "My rookie year, I'd go to the plate and not look at anyone or say anything to anyone. Joe [Joe West, veteran umpire] told me, 'You should say hello when you come up here.' Since my rookie year, I've done that. I don't want to do anything that's going to make an umpire mad at me."

Greet Your Coworkers

Here's a story that shows what can happen if you ignore your coworkers.

I was brought into an organization to teach assertiveness skills to salespeople. During the day, a number of administrative people complained that when the salespeople (who had come from the field and were unknown to them) walked into the coffee room, they did not acknowledge them. Yet as soon as the head sales manager walked into the room, the salespeople all said hello to him. The administrative people were insulted and furious: "Aren't we worth a hello?" And when one of the salespeople needed some work done . . . well, you know the rest of the story.

On the other hand, a temporary worker at a large corporation always greeted people as she went about her day, especially an employee she passed every morning. After a couple of weeks, he approached her and said, "You're so friendly. Let me have your résumé." He was director of HR and two weeks later she had a permanent full-time job. She now tells people, "I got my job because I said hello!"

Establishing Rapport with Strangers

You can establish rapport with strangers simply by offering a greeting in public places. Again, I am not talking about a dark alley, but why not say hello in line at the bank or the grocery store? I go to the post office fairly regularly in my town. Recently there was a new clerk and I said good morning to him. He looked at me with shock and surprise. "Oh, good morning to you!" he said back, clearly pleased that I had greeted him.

While I may not be looking to establish a close personal friendship with him, I'm a regular customer; he's a part of my day. He knows me and my son. He always goes out of his way to be pleasant, and when I mess up my shipping forms, he is understanding and helpful.

Once you try out this strategy of niceness, you will experience its benefits. Try planting a pleasant expression on your face. Smile and say hello. Give it a try. What a difference it makes in creating a pleasant mood.

But remember it's almost impossible to establish rapport with someone if you are on your phone. Put your phone down and connect with people.

2. Introduce Others

Another important component to establishing rapport and avoiding conflict is making introductions. Again, this seems simple. But it's amazing how often it gets botched. A lot of awkward and unnecessary tension is caused when people enter rooms or join conversations and are not introduced to one another. People don't make introductions, and then get upset when they in turn aren't introduced.

As I see it, people don't make introductions for three reasons.

- They don't realize it's their responsibility.

- They don't know how to do it properly.

- They forget the person's name.

But no matter what the reason, you need to make an introduction. In many ways, a poor introduction is better than no introduction.

The correct way to introduce a person in a professional or business setting is to mention the name of the person of importance or higher rank first, regardless of gender. It used to be that women's names were said first, but in the professional world this rule no longer applies. And if you don't know who has the highest position, then choose the person you want to flatter and mention that person's name first.

If you forget someone's name, just admit it. It happens to us all. In this embarrassing situation, lessen your own, and the other person's, discomfort by having a Polite and Powerful statement on the tip of your tongue. If you have just one line to remember, you are more apt to remember it and be more comfortable because you have something to say. Sample lines can be:

> I'm sorry. I've forgotten your name.
> Please excuse me; I can't recall your name.
> I know your face, but my mind's gone blank.
> I know your name, but please remind me.

Don't over-explain your lapse: "I can't remember your name because I'm so preoccupied and I was up so-o-o late last night." It happens to everyone. People understand that.

When you make introductions properly, you make others comfortable and that's a great step to make in establishing rapport and reducing conflict.

If Necessary, Introduce Yourself

Patrick and his coworker walked into a meeting. His coworker took the empty seat next to the vice president. A few minutes later, Patrick saw the coworker greet the VP and shake his hand. The two men spoke and appeared to connect.

Patrick later approached the coworker and said, "I thought you didn't know the VP."

"I didn't," he said, "but I decided to introduce myself."

As a result he made a connection with an important person in his company.

3. Everyone Needs to Shake Hands

Yet another greeting area that causes misunderstanding and interferes with establishing rapport has to do with the good old American handshake. We judge people based on the quality of their handshake and we make assumptions about them, often inviting conflict as a result.

Joanne made an assumption about her future brother-in-law. When she met him for the first time, he did not extend his hand to her. "Right away," she said, "I assumed he was sexist."

He wasn't sexist and the two eventually became friends. But what if this had been their only meeting? She would have made her assumption about him and it would have stuck. She would have walked away disgusted with him, while he would have had no idea why she seemed to want to get away from him so quickly.

Women make assumptions about other women based on the way they shake hands. One woman said about another woman's limp handshake, "Right away, I lost respect for her."

Men make assumptions too. I hear complaints from men who have gotten bone-crushing handshakes from other men, as if "he's showing me how tough he is."

Women with limp handshakes and men with crushing handshakes aren't necessarily wimps and bullies. They may not have been taught the proper rules of handshaking etiquette. Many people are unaware that they're shaking too softly or too firmly. People also get confused because there can be more than one set of rules that governs handshaking etiquette. There are rules for social behavior and rules for business behavior. Which rules apply for the handshake?

Social Etiquette Versus Business Etiquette

The handshake—or the lack of one—is the perfect example of how not understanding the evolving rules of business etiquette can cause conflict and have consequences. Here's an illustration to show you what I mean:

A senior VP walks into a meeting of three men and one woman. The three men stand up and shake hands with him. The woman does not stand up nor does she extend her hand. She may nod.

What assumption would you probably make about this woman? You would probably assume, as most people do, that the woman is not an equal or part of the group.

Depending upon our point of view, we can blame the man or the woman for this. Yet each is very possibly just following correct social behavior as taught. Many men, both young and old, were taught to wait for the woman to extend her hand. Many women were taught that they don't stand when being introduced. I was taught these rules. For years I did not rise for introductions or extend my hand to men or women. Finally I realized how much this action was holding me back from establishing rapport and making connections. As you can see from the example above, conflict can easily occur when certain social rules are carried over into the workplace.

In the olden days—unfortunately meaning my childhood—there were few women in the business world, and men and women rarely interacted in the business world. They interacted in the social world based on rules of etiquette. So when women started appearing in business in greater numbers, social rules spilled over into the workplace. Many men and women continued to follow the social rules of greetings.

Today, the rules of social etiquette don't apply in business and professional situations. We no longer make business etiquette decisions based on gender. Instead, we make them on rank and host/visitor status. The new guideline for shaking hands is that the higher-ranking person extends his or her hand first to welcome the other person. Give the higher-ranking person a split second, and if he or she doesn't extend the hand, you extend yours. The key is that the handshake needs to take place.

In a business and professional situation, both men and women should stand when shaking hands. Sometimes you might be caught off guard and you can't stand up in time. In that case you would lean forward and give the indication that you know you should be standing and you would, if you could.

A young woman recently asked me, "When did women start shaking hands?" I answered, "Every person, regardless of gender, should shake hands." Yet there are still many women who were never taught this guideline.

Other women are comfortable shaking hands with men but not with women. Often women are surprised when I come up to them and extend my hand. They're often not prepared to respond to my greeting.

Here's a story that underscores the importance of the handshake and your professional image. A creative director was told that she was hired in part because she shook hands with the interviewer at the beginning of the interview and at the end, which made her seem confident and professional. Her action turned out to be one of those deciding factors that can tip the scales in your favor when other things are equal.

Not Too Firm, Not Too Weak

In the United States, the handshake is the proper business protocol greeting. If you want to be taken seriously in business you *must* shake hands and you *must* shake properly.

To shake hands correctly:

1. Say your name and extend your hand.
2. Go in with the thumb up, at a slight angle. Make sure thumb joints meet.
3. It should be firm but not bone breaking. In the United States two or three pumps is enough.

You shake hands when you say hello and when you say good-bye. Of course there are exceptions. Some people have painful arthritis, or cultural reasons may prohibit them from shaking hands. If that is the case with you, simply say something like, "I'm so sorry. I am unable to shake hands."

What About Socially?

In social situations, should a woman extend her hand and shake? This is a good question and not easily answered. The social rules have also evolved in this area because more and more women are working and bringing handshake rules into the social world. Yet there are still many women who are not in the working world and don't know to shake hands or prefer to remain seated.

Often our greetings in social situations are more personal anyway. We often hug and kiss people we know well. I think that in social situations when new people are meeting, women should rise and shake hands. But again, many women and men may prefer the old way, so my guideline is this: take your cues from the situation and the people involved. And don't automatically assume someone is a jerk because his greeting protocol is different from yours.

Etiquette is like a dance, but it's not a waltz where every step is conveniently planned for you. You go with the flow and adjust as you go.

4. Don't Use Nicknames Without Permission

This is a short one compared with number three above, but it's important. Many people are very particular about what you do to their names. Some people will take offense if you greet them by a name they don't want to be called. It may not bother you whether you are called Robert or Rob, Jennifer or Jen, but other people do care:

- One man said that to make sure people don't use his nickname, he gives a preemptive modified WAC. When he greets people, he extends his hand and says, "My name is Richard; please don't call me Dick."

- A mechanic told me that other men always called him buddy or pal. This offended him.

- A friend of mine named Charles doesn't like people calling him Chuck. He refers to it as the "unauthorized shortening of my name." Though it may seem harmless to you, people can be very put off if you do this. In fact, Charles will not do business with people who call him Chuck.

Why risk offending someone by using a nickname? If the person has a name that is typically shortened, like Patty for Patricia or Bob for Robert, ask the person what he or she wants to be called.

If you need to WAC someone because she's calling you by a nickname, keep it simple and just give your A. "I prefer to be called Patricia."

5. Know the New Rules of Helping Etiquette

Helping etiquette is another illustration of social etiquette potentially causing conflict in the workplace. It used to be that men were expected to do helping things for women, like opening the door, letting her order first, paying the bill, pulling her chair out, and assisting her with her coat.

But like the rules of greetings, the rules of helping etiquette have also changed significantly in the workplace. If a man "helps" a woman with her coat, pays her bill for a business lunch, pulls out her chair at a board meeting, and so on, the image created is one of a dependent woman who needs to be taken care of. In the workplace today, this is not the image women want if they expect to be considered competent, credible, and powerful.

In business and professional situations, women should not expect men to do these things for them. But what about socially? Again what you choose to do socially is no longer guided by hard and fast dos and don'ts. And yes, it can be confusing. As I explained before, you can be in a social situation where the person is applying the rules of business etiquette.

Couples work out how much helping etiquette they are comfortable with in their relationships. I like my husband to help me with my coat. He likes helping me with my coat. So this is what we do. It's our choice.

Yet I do not expect men in business to help me with my coat or open doors for me unless my arms are full. Which brings me to the point that helping etiquette, regardless of gender, should be guided by one simple principle: help anyone who needs help. If a man is having trouble negotiating his arm into his coat, what should a woman do? Stand there and laugh at him or ignore him? Of course not. She should help him with his coat.

Raul was being courted by several investment firms for a regional director's position. After one interview, the VP who had been meeting with him helped Raul with his heavy coat. Raul said that gesture helped him decide in favor of that company.

Should You WAC the Helper?

Some women get upset when men try to help them. Instead of jumping to the conclusion that a man is sexist, give him the jerk test first (Chapter 5). It really is possible that the man waiting for you to exit the elevator is doing what he thinks is expected of him, or he's simply being nice. Yelling at him or storming out of the elevator is not Polite and Powerful behavior. You can simply say thank-you and let it go at that. I personally feel I would be inviting more conflict into my life by challenging every man I have met in an elevator who allowed me to exit first. Am I really bothered if a man I don't know at a corporation I'm visiting for a day holds a door for me? No. But if you have a colleague who always insists on helping you, you can choose to WAC the person:

Your W (What's bothering you): "I know you're just being nice, yet when you continually open doors for me, pull out my chair, help me with my coat, and pay the bill at lunch, I believe it creates the impression that I'm dependent on you or that I can't take care of myself."

Your A (What do you want to ask the person to do): In the future, if I need help I'll ask you.

Your C (Check in with the other person): Okay?

You can also adapt your WAC'em, which I prefer, and keep it shorter: "Thanks. I appreciate the offer, but I can handle it myself."

"But I Insist!"

Some men still want to follow social rules in business situations. This may be fine, a courtesy or kindness here and there. But if you're a man, beware of overdoing it. You may invite conflict by continually helping a woman who doesn't want help.

6. Know How to Make Small Talk

After you say hello, get introduced, and shake hands, what do you do next? If you want to establish a relationship with a person you don't know, you should engage that person in conversation—even if you think you're bad at engaging in small talk.

You may be shy. The unfortunate truth is that sometimes in our society we judge shyness harshly—she's stuck up or he thinks he's so important—when in reality these people are sweating it out just as much the next person.

If you're shy or prone to get tongue-tied, you should challenge yourself to overcome this condition. The ability to make small talk is a crucial skill to develop in business and helpful in everyday life. It helps you establish and maintain rapport.

I believe that I was accepted into a graduate program on merit, but my admission was helped along because I had established rapport with the dean's secretary. After we had chatted a few times she had said to me, "I made sure your papers were seen by the dean."

If you are among those not endowed with the gift of the gab, there are ways you can compensate. Believe me, I've seen tongue-tied people learn to become fluent in the language of small talk. The ability to make small talk is a skill that can be learned. Here are some suggestions:

1. Ask questions to draw out the other person and create a two-way conversation.
2. If appropriate, refer to the last time the two of you were together.
3. Try to find out what the other person's interests are.
4. Watch your use of buzzwords and expressions that others might not understand.
5. Avoid controversial subjects like politics, religion, ethics, and the like. I am not advocating superficiality. I am advocating getting to know people better first before you start debating with them on sensitive issues. Good small-talk topics include trends in your field, the weather, movies, books, sports (if all are interested), the environment you are in, and so forth.
6. Know your nonverbal skills. Review the guidelines stated in Chapter 8. While you're engaging in small talk, don't look at your phone or text, or cross your arms. Smile. Make eye contact. Listen and show that you are listening. People sense whether someone is genuinely interested or not.

7. Pay Sincere Attention to Others

A sincere interest in others has always been important to establishing rapport. But now smartphones and computer screens often pull your attention away from the person you're with. Research shows that even a phone on the table inhibits conversation. So talk all you want, shake hands all you want, but you can't connect and build relationships with people unless you give them your sincere and undivided attention. People want to know that you're listening to them. You can't listen if you're trying to read a text, typing on a keyboard, or answering the phone.

I'm amazed that I have to tell people, "Don't answer your phone or check your screen when someone is in your home or office." This is very rude. Taking a call while you're already engaged in a conversation is a fast and sure way to let someone know that she isn't as important as the person who may be calling. This is why there is voice mail. I was told of a managing partner in a law firm who took phone calls when a client was meeting in his office. Until he read my etiquette book, he had no clue that he was being rude. And this man has a law degree and a PhD.

I know, I know. There are times you must answer your phone, but you should explain why: "I've been expecting this call. It's from my doctor." Then do your business and get off the phone as quickly as possible.

Sophia visited a sick friend who received a call from another friend and proceeded to talk to her for twenty minutes. Sophia became upset with her friend, understandably. It would have made me think that her other friend (who wasn't even there) was more important than me.

This problem of inattention isn't limited to phones and computer screens. A man told me that he was interviewing with an executive who opened his mail during the interview. He ended up being offered the job but not taking it: "Who wants to report to a person who doesn't seem to care that I exist?" I wouldn't want to work for a person like that either.

8. Don't Interrupt Others

This is an item that appears on the list in Chapter 1. Many people consider it one of the most annoying of all the annoying habits, and it can significantly interfere with your ability to establish rapport, so I am highlighting it again here. People don't know they are interrupting, and don't know what to say when it happens to them. As a result conflicts can occur. People will not want to have more conversations with you. They may avoid you. You can't build relationships if people see you and head the other way.

Don't interrupt me when I'm interrupting you.

—WINSTON CHURCHILL

You may be an interrupter.
"You mean me?"

Yes, you! A lot of people don't realize they're interrupting until it's pointed out to them. It's become an ingrained habit. Of course, people do occasionally interrupt one another, but when it becomes a regular pattern it is bothersome. This is the man no one wants on their team because he keeps interrupting during meetings. He has no clue. If you catch yourself mouthing the words that you think the other person is going to say, then you may have this problem.

I heard about an energetic book discussion group that made a rule: You can't speak until at least five other people have given their opinion. This is a great rule. Practice it whenever you're in a group discussion.

ON YOUR OWN

What will you say or do when someone interrupts you? I encourage you to come up with a Polite and Powerful line. You'll get used to saying it and it works. You could try to continue talking and give the person a hint that way, but there are people who don't get hints. Here are some possibilities:

I'll be happy to address that as soon as I finish my thought.

I'll discuss that as soon as I am finished.

Hold that thought.

---

9. Use Humor Wisely

I don't want to get into a discussion of political correctness and humor. That's not what this book is about. It is about how to get along with others and how to deal with conflict when it arises. Therefore, be cautious with humor when building rapport. You're not going to get along with others if you go around telling jokes that offend them.

When I talk about this subject, people always groan. Then the story-telling starts: "My friend is always telling the grossest jokes." They groan because the inappropriate jokes annoy them.

Humor can be an effective communication tool or you can bomb badly with it. Humor can be difficult to pull off because what is funny to one person may not be to another. And something that is intended to be funny may hurt or put down other people and invite conflict. I don't want to ban jokes, but I do think people would be wise to be judicious in how they unleash what they think is humorous.

It May Seem Like Just a Joke to You

Telling inappropriate stories or off-color jokes is not okay. There are loads of people out there who don't understand the consequences, which is why I want to share this next story.

On the first day of a new semester, a man in my MBA class told a dirty joke during his presentation. I WAC'ed him for it. I told him it was inappropriate. He was furious with me. He accused me of being politically correct and no fun. Yet the following week, he said he noticed that he was telling those types of stories more than he had thought. And he had been mad at management for not considering him a viable candidate for promotion. By the end of the semester he had written me a letter:

"The first day of class made me realize that the way I presented myself was largely responsible for why I had not been considered a serious candidate [for promotion]. My behavior contributed to the way they [peers and supervisors] responded to me and in turn, contributed to my poor attitude in the plant.

"I began to make a conscious effort to change some of the things that were bogging me down. At first I really didn't want to believe that these things were the cause for my failure to get noticed in the company. But I realized quickly that they did.

"It was about three months after the first day of class that I was offered the position of die shop superintendent."

Humor Must Not Be Cruel

Have you ever met a person who continuously makes fun of others—their profession, religion, culture, personal quirks, ethnic background, and so on? Besides the fact that it makes the speaker look bad, it can make the other person feel bad. It just isn't nice!

A man went into a potential client's office and noticed a picture of the man, his wife, and their six kids. He said, "Good Catholic, eh?" The potential client decided not to do business with him based solely on that comment.

When Humor Works

Don't be humorous but do have a sense of humor. Humor can be used to diffuse difficult situations from developing. It can stop you from taking a situation too seriously.

One morning my mom was visiting during the coldest winter on record. It was about 10 degrees outside and I was getting my son ready for preschool. She looked at me and said, "Barbara, don't forget to put on Jacob's jacket." I said to her, "Thanks Mom, I am sure I was about to let him out of the house without it!" She laughed and got my point.

After someone asks a ridiculous personal question, you can respond with humor to get your point across without actually WAC'ing the person:

"I'll forgive you for asking if you forgive me for not answering."

A man asked a woman, "Are you still pregnant?" She replied, "No, I am carrying this for a friend who is on vacation."

The most important etiquette guideline for humor is to remember that what you may find hilarious someone else may find offensive.

10. Be Polite

It is time to reengineer kindness back into our everyday lives. One very simple way to do this is to use polite words. I remind people—because I have to—to use polite words in corporate America, just as I had to when I lectured in my son's elementary school.

Doing so in business, at school, and in everyday life will help you with new relationships as well as established ones.

These are simple words, such as thank-you, please, excuse me, and I'm sorry.

If you bump into someone and don't excuse yourself, the other person may become angry with you. You invite conflict into your life by not acknowledging the bump. If you say thank-you to someone, she is more likely to help you in the future.

A job hunter asked a recruiter to call a company and put in a good word for him. She did. He got the job. He never called to thank her. She was insulted. She told me she would never help him again.

The Power of Polite Language

The manager who uses polite language with his administrative person is more apt to accomplish what he wants. The customer who says please to the clerk is more likely to have a pleasant exchange than a nasty one. Though I say thank-you to the ticket machine on the New Jersey turnpike, it doesn't influence the outcome!

Using polite words also means no cursing and no sexist or racist language. You can instantly turn people off from wanting to get to know you. You may mean no harm but you can still do harm. You can offend people and appear aggressive.

11. Be Considerate

When I ask people what drives them nuts at work, I hear the word "inconsiderate" quite a lot. This is the person who:

- Doesn't refill the paper in the copy machine. But do let people jump in line if they only have one copy to make and you have three hundred.

- Breaks office equipment and doesn't let anyone know it needs to be fixed.

- Leaves a teaspoon of coffee in the pot for the next person. Is it so hard to make a pot of coffee?

- Lets uneaten food turn into a science experiment. Remove your old food from the refrigerator. Clean up after yourself.

- Leaves empty soda cans or coffee cups on the meeting room table for someone else to clean up.

- Doesn't respect the privacy of others. Don't listen in on phone conversations, read things on other people's desks, or post private information about people online.

- Borrows things and doesn't return them. And don't borrow things from someone's desk when that person is not there.

- Plays loud music (even through ear buds) or makes loud, distracting phone calls.

Review this list. Make sure you're not the person doing these things.

You spend a good portion of each day with your coworkers. You should, therefore, make every effort to share the work space considerately. If you are not considerate with people at work, they may avoid you. They may see you coming and think, "Oh no, here comes that Tony; he never makes a pot of coffee." Wouldn't you hate to be Tony?

Respect Your Neighbor's Space

You share a property line with each neighbor and you respect that line. But the space you share with your neighbors extends beyond a fence or driveway. You can reach into another person's space with loud music and loud voices. I once lived near a family with teenagers. They were a nice family except the kids were loud. They yelled a lot in the yard, they played loud music, and one of them played the drums at 10:00 or 11:00 PM. At first I thought the noise would stop soon because it had to be driving the parents crazy too. Apparently not!

This is a good example of why we sometimes do not WAC people. We think "they must know this is bothersome behavior." Yet in reality they often don't know. I ended up WAC'ing my neighbors. They were surprised when I told them I could hear the drums as clearly as if they were being played next to me. They were apologetic and suggested different times for their son to practice.

Though I still heard the drums occasionally at night, at least it wasn't late at night. It could have been worse—much worse. I have heard horror stories about nightmare neighbors. I have heard stories about parents who don't properly supervise their kids, who walk their dog on everyone's property, who use the next door neighbor's garden as a shortcut, and more. These are simply rude actions. Behaving rudely back only makes things worse. Sometimes people don't realize they're bothering you. So speak up. Just make sure you do it Politely and Powerfully.

12. Be Aware of Cultural Differences

In Chapter 5, the "jerk" chapter, we considered cultural differences that may cause conflict. You may be thinking, "I'm not going anywhere; I don't need to know these things."

But you do. You do because you may travel abroad for work or pleasure. You may encounter a visitor or a colleague from another country. You may engage with an international coworker via Skype, phone, or email. If we don't understand the cultural differences, we are quick to put a negative spin on the person's behavior. It's easy to think the person is a "jerk" for many mistaken reasons. This can be an area of major conflict.

An American pharmaceutical VP met his counterpart from Japan. When he received the man's business card, he proceeded to pick his teeth with it. That's considered rude behavior in the United States, but very offensive in Japan. This executive made a bad impression and damaged their working relationship.

Etiquette varies from culture to culture. Of course, culture is just one of the many contributing factors to behavior. Others include personality style, gender, age, religion, education, and the organizational climate in which the person works. Therefore, there are no absolutes; every rule for international etiquette is likely to have an exception.

But there is one basic guideline that can help you navigate the globe—literally. If you're the traveler you must adapt. Just as we expect visitors to our country to adopt our customs, you are expected to figure out how to function in another country. After all, you are the one who is doing the touring if you're on vacation. If you're traveling for work, you're representing your company. This means you must read and study before you go. Many culture-specific guidebooks, websites, and travel agents are available to tell you about the particular customs of the country you are visiting. Talk to people who have lived or worked in that culture. Find someone you trust and ask questions. The more you know the easier you will be able to adapt.

Avoiding Cultural Differences in Your Own Backyard

If you're at home, you're in your own culture. You aren't technically required to adapt or change your behavior. However, I encourage you to be open-minded when you encounter cultural differences. Life will be more interesting and less stressful if you do. As a general rule, when you're interacting with someone from a different cultural background or country, before you assume the person is a jerk, assume that the difficulty you may be experiencing stems from a difference in culture or custom. Here are four additional guidelines you should follow:

1. Don't React Negatively to Different Customs

A Brazilian woman who had just come to the United States kissed me good-bye right after meeting me. I was taken aback but kissed her cheek too.

If someone doesn't know or follow our customs, don't react with hostility. He should make every effort to adapt, true, but it may take time. The person may not have the same resources you do and may not have the same desire to avoid conflict.

But what if you're really bothered by something your international colleague or friend does while visiting? You can speak up and communicate your discomfort. Just do it Politely and Powerfully:

- Be discreet. Don't correct someone publicly. Take him aside and discreetly WAC him: "I'm sure you have no idea (softening statement) that men usually don't hug each other in corporate America (what's bothering you). I don't mind because I know you, but it would be better if you made a habit of just shaking hands (what you've asked him to do). Okay?" (check in).

- Don't insult. You're not putting down anyone's custom, you're simply informing him of ours. Don't say anything harsh, such as: "We wouldn't dare do such a thing here!" Be polite and sensitive about it. More positive wording for your W would be: "It is customary in the US to wait in line."

- Follow up. Check in with the person to see how she is managing. Make yourself available. Be helpful and supportive. Become a mentor. Answer any questions the person may have about American culture. If you are hosting an international visitor, it's your responsibility to help her adapt and be comfortable.

2. Understand Nonverbal Differences

By now you know the importance of having control over your nonverbal messages. It's especially important to understand nonverbal messages that vary from culture to culture.

Eye contact, for example, is a nonverbal difference that often causes confusion or conflict. In many Asian cultures averting the eyes is considered a sign of respect. Yet in the United States we don't trust people who look away from us. We may think they're sneaky, shifty, hiding something. "That jerk is just plain not listening to me!"

I know a head nurse at an American hospital who was working with an Asian doctor on a project. They met weekly. The nurse was getting increasingly annoyed because the doctor did not look at her. She thought she didn't value her because she was a nurse. One day she exploded at the doctor, "Who do you think you are? You think you are better than I am. The least you can do is show me some respect and look at me when we are talking."

The doctor looked up and said, "But I am showing you respect in my culture." (This nurse felt like a jerk. A big one!)

3. Be Sensitive About Language Differences

I have a Belgian friend who said that he was a slow learner. He didn't learn his fifth language until he was twenty-two!

While it's true that people all over the world speak English, especially international businesspeople who speak our language quite well, you need to appreciate that it's usually their second or third language. We can be very critical of those who do not speak English well. Yet we may be able to speak only one language.

My Polish friend and I decided to help each other learn the other's language. I said to her one day, "Polish is so hard!" She looked at me in surprise and said, "English is so hard." I stopped complaining.

You may need to speak more slowly but not more loudly when conversing with someone for whom English is not the primary language. Americans who shout at people who are speaking English as a second language are showing their own lack of knowledge.

4. Remember That Polite and Powerful Is an International Language

No matter where on earth you travel, if you are Polite and Powerful within the context of each culture you travel to, you will be a happier and less stressed traveler.

When you meet an international visitor who does not adhere to our customs, give the person the benefit of the doubt. He is probably not a jerk. If you have a relationship with the person, try to help him adapt.

Start Doing These Twelve Simple Things Today

While I don't encourage you to put this book down and go out and WAC your boss your first time out of the positive confrontation gate, I do encourage you to start practicing these twelve ways to avoid conflict—immediately. They are all easy to implement (though the handshake and small talk skills may take you a little time), and you will begin to reap the benefits right away.

And don't forget . . . give yourself a chance. It may take time to learn new behaviors and you may occasionally err, but if your effort is sincere, that will count in your favor. Establishing rapport will ultimately say that you are a respectful, gracious, and Polite and Powerful person. You are the kind of person I want to do business with or would be happy to meet in my neighborhood.

Conclusion: A Final Pep Talk

Congratulations! You're no longer a pretender, avoider, complainer, displacer, self-discounter, bully, or shouter. But you may be wondering how to get started as a Polite and Powerful person. We've covered a lot of ground about positive confrontation and conflict avoidance in these pages. It's a lot to learn, yes. What should you do first?

Take your time—you don't have to learn and implement everything in this book overnight. (All along, I've cautioned you against running out the door with your WAC'em arms flapping. Don't fly into work tomorrow, swoop down, and WAC your boss.) Work your way up to the big ones.

Here's an eleven-step plan to help you get started:

1. Start where the book starts—with self-awareness. Take a few days and tune in to who you are as a confronter and a communicator. You don't have to do anything other than think and reflect. Keep a journal—even a small memo pad will do. Writing down things you realize about yourself for a few days will help you pinpoint your areas for improvement. Review the self-assessment exercise on page 31. Tell yourself, "I'm tired of being a bully (or a displacer, or a pretender, etc.); it's time to change." Make a point to review your use of social media. Is it contributing to the conflict in your life?

2. Focus on your confrontational style and the communication skills you feel you may need the most immediate help with—whether it

be not shouting at others when you get upset or standing without crossing your feet or crossing your arms. Practice—you can break bad habits. I have seen people think "I can't" and yet they do.

3. Before you decide to confront someone, give that person the jerk test. Does she really mean you harm? Review the reasons given in Chapter 5 that may be causing the conflict. Is this one to let go?

4. If you decide to have a confrontation, prepare your WAC'em wording. Review all the steps in Chapter 6. Once you have your WAC'em wording right, review the eleven simple things you can do to make your confrontation positive. Role-play with a friend.

5. Believe that you can have a positive confrontation.

6. Come up with an exit line in case the confrontation starts to go downhill, so that you can get out of the room. You can always WAC another day. Just say, "I can see this isn't a good time; let's talk again later" or "I'm getting a little worked up; I'll pick this up with you later."

7. Use your WAC'em card, as described in Chapter 6, to help you review your W, A, and C before your difficult conversation starts. Keep it in your wallet or purse so that you can pull it out in case of emergency.

8. Take inventory of how you did and what you will do differently in the future. Do not expect perfection of yourself, in the beginning or ever. The power of positive confrontation is a skill you can learn. You can get better at it—and you will.

9. Follow up with the other person. You won't change overnight and the person you WAC won't either.

10. Once you feel comfortable in the world of positive confrontation, make an effort to reduce potential conflict in your life. Review your rapport-building skills.

11. Enjoy the benefits of positive confrontation. You will be able to let things go. You will feel better about yourself. You will improve your relationships with others. You won't waste time avoiding or dreading difficult conversations.

I Want to Hear From You

Send me your success stories so that I can share them with others. You'll also find additional information, tips, and advice on my website, www. pachter.com; my Facebook page, www.facebook.com/pachtertraining; and Twitter, @barbarapachter. You can also sign up for my blog, Pachter's Pointers, www.barbarapachtersblog.com.

Like the many men and women I've taught Polite and Powerful behavior to over the past twenty years, you are now set to enjoy the benefits of living a less stressed out, conflict-free life.

Good luck.

ABOUT THE AUTHORS

Barbara Pachter, MA, is an internationally renowned business etiquette and communications speaker, coach, and author. She has delivered more than 2,100 seminars throughout the world, including the first-ever seminar for businesswomen in Kuwait. Pachter is also adjunct faculty in the School of Business at Rutgers University.

Her client list boasts many of today's most notable organizations, including Bayer HealthCare, Campbell Soup, Children's Hospital of Philadelphia, Chrysler, Cisco Systems, Cleveland Clinic, Con Edison, Microsoft, Novartis, Pfizer, Princeton University, and Wawa.

Pachter is the author of ten books, including *The Essentials of Business Etiquette: How to Greet, Eat, and Tweet Your Way to Success* and *When the Little Things Count . . . And They Always Count.* Her books have been translated into eleven languages.

She is quoted regularly in newspapers and magazines, including the *Wall Street Journal,* the *New York Times, Time,* and *Oprah Magazine,* and she has appeared on ABC's *20/20, The Today Show,* and *The Early*

Show. Her discussion of business etiquette appeared in the *Harvard Business Review.*

Pachter's areas of expertise include assertive communication, positive confrontation, business etiquette, presentation skills, business writing, business dress, career suggestions, and women in the workplace. She holds undergraduate and graduate degrees from the University of Michigan, and completed postgraduate studies in the Middle East and at Temple University. She has taught English as a second language (ESL).

Barbara Pachter can be reached at:
Pachter & Associates
P.O. Box 3680
Cherry Hill, NJ 08034, USA
Telephone: (856) 751–6141
Email: bpachter@pachter.com
www.pachter.com

To connect with Pachter via social media:
www.facebook.com/pachtertraining
www.barbarapachtersblog.com
www.linkedin.com/in/barbarapachter
www.twitter.com/barbarapachter

Susan Magee, MFA, is an assistant professor of communications and the author or coauthor of several nonfiction books. She lives in Philadelphia with her husband and son.